CLASSIC CRI

KING OF THE LAGS

The Story of CHARLES PEACE

by

DAVID WARD

Foreword
by
Richard Whittington-Egan

SOUVENIR PRESS

First published by
ELEK BOOKS LTD.

This Edition first published 1989 by
SOUVENIR PRESS LTD,
43 Great Russell Street,
London, WC1B 3PA
and simultaneously in Canada

ISBN 0285 629093 hardback
ISBN 0 285 629107 paperback

Printed in Great Britain by
Billing & Sons Ltd, Worcester

FOREWORD

It is precisely one hundred and ten years since swagman Charlie Peace, brimful of religious cant and rant to the judicially appointed end, was 'turned off' by Mr Hangman Marwood to the pulpit-thump of the gallows' trap at Armley Gaol, in Leeds.

A blackguard died, took, in his own words, 'a short cut to Heaven' via the scaffold — and another folk-hero was born. Henceforth generations of street children would chant his funeral orisons to the measured swish and beat of skipping-ropes:

> I love Charlie.
> Charlie was a thief,
> Charlie killed a copper,
> Charlie came to grief.

Thus, out of popular sentiment, did an improper Charlie become a 'wery partickler' one, the romanticised scion of such precedent outsider heroes as Dick Turpin and Jack Sheppard. Crowned King of Lags, monarch of the 'penny dreadfuls', he was canonised to tarnished immortality. His name, permitted to grace no Christian stone, was secularly enshrined alongside those of Jack the Ripper and Dr Crippen to complete the unholy trinity in the black Pantheon of popularly celebrated criminals.

Charles Peace was the Great Dissembler. Chameleonine. Protean. Polymorphous. Skin stained with walnut juice, beard tethered in with cunning bands, he was by turns a harmless old woman, a beaming clergyman, or a jolly Captain-Hook-armed sailor. Jaw dislocated — he had the 'gift' of being able to snap it out at will — plasticine-faced, unchallengeable champion of chin-to-nose 'nurdlers', he was safely beyond recognition. White-headed, sunken-eyed behind wire-framed spectacles, dwarfish and delicate in physique, coughing and piping feebly, he became an amiable old buffer.

To capture so amoebiform a creature on paper must have been almost as taxing as it had proved to net the flesh-and-blood original. But Mr Ward has, in this, the only full, factual, modern biographical account of the Victorian super-Sykes, most brilliantly succeeded.

The nature of Peace was complex. Quintessentially the product of his time and place, Victorian urban England of the dark satanic mills, he was a kind of grimy hobgoblin of the Industrial Revolution. A loner, a Wilsonian, bred-in-the-gland outsider, pursuing his outcast's career with what in any other context one might dub Smilesian virtue, he became the most successful burglar of Victorian times. Yet there was also much of the modern villain about him. He would have made a good fourth at the Krays' bridge table.

The image is complicated. There is Peace seen, as it were, through the magic lantern: a caricature almost — striped jersey, flat cap, black face-mask, carrying dark-lantern and swag bag, the very model of the voracious-jawed larval stage of the mature gentleman of the broad arrow. There is Peace — or, rather, Mr John Thompson — the respected tenant of respectable Evelina Road, Peckham or Nunhead, the parlour Christian, family man, genial host at religiously regular musical 'At Homes', keen churchgoer, erratic Sunday school teacher, enthusiastic violinist, animal lover, and ardent pacifist. Such was the charity of this domesticated paragon that he would even provide an impecunious milkman with free stabling for his horse. What the milkman did not know was that kind Mr Thompson worked the poor horse on his nocturnal bourgeois-milking rounds, and the cob's owner was consequently much puzzled by the animal's diurnal sluggishness.

There exists, too, the extraordinary physical, as well as psychical, dichotomy between the blameless old gentleman with the frail, bowed shoulders and the crippled leg, and the mischievous little monkey of a creature, shinning up drainpipes and, propelled by apelike strength, able to leap and lope across rooftops, bound on errands of larceny and creating a one-man crime wave that terrorised the big houses of Peckham, Camberwell, Lewisham, Blackheath and Greenwich.

It was as a fourteen-year-old, working in a steel rolling mill in his native Sheffield, that Peace, discovering the rewards of honest toil — permanent laming by a piece of red hot steel which entered his leg just below the knee — elected his own brand of self-help, a life of crime. Beginning humbly enough as a pickpocket, he graduated in the course of many spells of time to what used to be quaintly termed a portico thief: that is, a housebreaker who specialises in climbing in via the porch. We would call it a cat burglar today. He carried the tools of his trade — a goodly bunch of skeleton keys, a few hundred yards of strong, thin cord, a couple of wedges, a gimlet, a jemmy and a revolver of the bulldog type — in a violin case, thus anticipating the custom later adopted by the suzerains of Mr Capone's Chicago. He also constructed a highly ingenious folding ladder to aid his ascents in his illicit profession. It is to this day in the safe-keeping of the Black Museum at Scotland Yard.

Literally light fingered — one missing from his left hand — he adroitly contrived to conceal his give-away maimed hand with a false lower arm of leather and wood, functionally furnished with a terminal bent-screw hook. That, too, rests *in pace* in a glass case in the Black Museum.

Peace early learned the lesson of temperance when a surfeit of whisky sent him, apprehended through fuddle-headed carelessness, to the hulks. He learned, too, essential callousness. When the exigency of one of life's dangerous corners compelled, he could without qualm or let take human life. He could — and did — sit flint-hearted in court and witness the sentencing of a man to death for a murder which he had committed — and then go out and do another *the very next day*.

All this and much more Mr Ward has skilfully brought forward in evidence, and he has most effectively set his bizarre anti-hero against the tell-tale background of the unique era that bore and shaped this maleficent sprite. He has captured the weird duality of mild, white-haired, bespectacled and benevolent 'genteelity' ill-sitting at one and the same time with something rank and goatish about the man. Odd, too, was the way in which, almost from his teens, Peace managed to project the air and ethos of the aged. Shrunken and etiolated, seemingly in his sixties when they hanged him, he was in fact only in his forty-seventh year.

To the last-of-all scene which Mr Ward limns for us I would like to add an eerie, post-mortem glimpse. It was vouchsafed, he believes, to Michael Martin-Harvey, son of the great actor-manager. Himself an actor, he was playing the leading rôle in a film of the life and death of Charlie Peace. He was sitting in the death cell, handling the original model of a cathedral which Peace was said to have carved while awaiting execution, and which had been generously lent to the film company by Madame Tussaud's. He was, he remembers, gently touching the spire of the cathedral when, quite suddenly, he felt a horny palm being placed over his hand. Fingers, hard and sinewy, inserted themselves between his, squeezing them tightly. On a number of occasions during the filming he had been conscious of a presence; now he was absolutely certain *whose* it had been.

Was Mr Ward ever, one wonders, perhaps in the small, dark hours of a long, late writing session, made uncomfortably conscious of a hovering presence at his busy elbow? It would not surprise me if it were so, for in this excellent book, now made deservedly available once more, he has most uncannily summoned back from the eternal time traveller's whirling spheres artful old Charlie's unpeaceful shade.

RICHARD WHITTINGTON-EGAN

ACKNOWLEDGMENTS

A great many people helped me while I was preparing and writing this book. My sincere thanks are due pre-eminently to my wife, to Miss Ann Lee of Elek Books, and to Mr. Richard Whittington-Egan.

Among others I would like to mention with gratitude are:

Mr. Robert Gray and Mr. W. Donald Cowley of Messrs Clegg and Sons, Solicitors, Sheffield; Mr. D. C. Cooper of George Newnes Ltd; Mr. T.P. Watson, Editor of the *Star*, Sheffield; Mr. Ludovic Kennedy; The Chief Constable of Lancashire, Colonel T. E. St. Johnston C.B.E., and Inspector Jackson, of Lancashire County Constabulary; Mrs. H. Walker, daughter of the late Rev. J. H. Littlewood, one-time Vicar of Darnall; Mr. Arthur Moyse, of London; Mrs. A. Stocks, of Bridlington; Mrs. E. Waddington, of Leeds; Lady Josephine Hobson; Mr. M. Fleming, of Spennymoor, Co. Durham; The Chief Constable of Sheffield and Chief Superintendent George A. Carnill, of Sheffield City Police; Mr. Samuel Holker, of Stretford; Mr. J. Henry, of Horsforth, Leeds; Mr. P. M. Beard, Barrister-at-Law, of Sheffield; Mrs. H. E. Partridge, of Exeter; Mr. James Green, of Manchester; Mr. A. F. Williams, of Manchester; Mr. C. Cowen, of the *Guardian*, Manchester; The City Librarian and Information Officer, and his staff, of Sheffield; The City Engineer of Sheffield; Mr. W. Dunkley, of Santon, Isle of Man; Mr. Hugh Pitt; The Chief Commissioner of New Scotland Yard and Mr. Dawson, Curator of the Black Museum at Scotland Yard; The Chief Constable of Manchester and Chief Superintendent F. W. Hughes, of Manchester City Police; Mr. John Clapp, Borough Engineer and Surveyor of Camberwell, London; The Editors of the *Yorkshire Post*, the *Yorkshire Evening Post*, the *Guardian*, the *Spectator*, the *Manchester Evening News*; Mr. Cartney, of Madame Tussauds, London; and a special word of thanks to Mr. H. G. Pearson, Departmental Record Officer, Home Office; Mr. R. L. Storey, of the Public Record Office; Dr. and Mrs. R. W. L. Ward, of Sprotborough, near Doncaster, also Mr. and Mrs. E. Clarkson, of Sprotborough.

There were others too numerous to set out here, but I would like any of them who happen to read this book to know that I was appreciative of their kindness to a stranger.

D.W.

"He was a demon beyond the power of Shakespeare to paint."

—*a former mistress.*

"He spoke happily as though the Condemned Cell was the shortest route to Paradise."

—*Prison Chaplain.*

CHAPTER ONE

ONE AUTUMN evening an ugly but intensely vital little man sat in his drawing-room singing hymns in praise of God and all His gifts. Often he had prayed that He would make things happen for His servant's good. And indeed He had. He had, for example, granted His servant the great cleverness that had enabled him to win through to the social prosperity and domestic felicity for which he had craved during a stormy life. This Deity was a Victorian English God—a tough-minded, socially conscious Omnipotence who offered material rewards to those who helped themselves.

Mr. John Thompson, respected citizen of the respectable suburb of Peckham in South London, was a happy man as he raised his voice in evangelical song at a musical "At Home" in his semi-detached villa, 5 East Terrace, Evelina Road. Outside the warm blustery winds of October 10th, 1878, made the widely-spaced gas lamps flicker wildly in the dark streets, but behind the villa's tight-drawn venetian blinds the gaslight shone cheerfully on the well-polished suite of expensive walnut furniture, the gilded mirrors and the dainty china and rich silverware bearing the remains of a solid tea of cake and ham and shrimps and winkles and watercress.

Neighbours who had attended the musical *soirées* that were such a feature of Mr. Thompson's home smiled in tolerant approval as they heard the sounds of music. They could visualize the scene.

Tonight only the family were present, so there would be Mr. Thompson, elderly and benevolent of aspect, comfortable in beaded slippers with his favourite violin at hand, ready to oblige with an air. His buxom and much younger wife, Sue, would be a richly-gowned and well-favoured figure at the bijou piano. Fervently joining in the songs would be the couple's lodger, Mrs. Ward, a drab but worthy figure in widow's weeds, and her young son Willie. Willie did odd jobs for Mr. Thompson, who had taught him to accompany the voices on a guitar.

Perhaps later Mr. Thompson would be persuaded to give one of his recitations—the gravedigger's scene from Hamlet was a great favourite—or one of the songs of which he was fond, such as the elevating ditty which began:

> "Oh would that we had Charity
> For every man and woman"

and ended:—

> "Then let us banish jealousy,
> Let's lift our fallen brother,
> And as we journey down life's road
> Be good to one another."

Maybe Mrs. Thompson would be prepared to "render" in her sweet and controlled voice one of the sentimental ballads to which Victorians were so partial. A treat that, if company were present, would occasion her husband to wipe his eyes and exclaim, "That was lovely, pet," and to explain with fond proprietorship that his Sue had once been the pride of many church choirs.

However swiftly the evening sped by with these harmless pleasures, one thing was certain. All noise would cease around 10 p.m. Mr. Thompson was known to disapprove of late nights and unseemly behaviour.

Like most of his middle-class acquaintances Mr. Thompson believed in presenting a decorous facade to the world. The pendulum had swung from the turbulence of the early years of the century, when the great explosion of industrial development had scattered over the land wealth for some, but riot and disorder for the less fortunate. This was now a society organising itself in its newfound wealth and sense of Imperial purpose. It felt somewhat self-conscious about the Old Adam which it feared might still lurk below the surface.

Mr. Thompson, however, was not a man of self-doubt. He felt only complacency that his enterprise and application had created for him such a comfortable niche in this rich society.

Rich indeed it might be, but it was one in which a man

had to know how to look after himself and his family. *The Times* that very morning had carried several columns of advertisements for domestic servants such as "Plain cook wanted, aged about 25, four in family, two other servants kept." It had also recorded that in London alone in the first week of October there were 76,767 paupers, half of them homeless, many of them young children.

Mr. Thompson had been in Manchester during the winter earlier in the year. It had been one of exceptional severity. Police Superintendent James Bent—whom Mr. Thompson knew well by sight—had been walking home one January night of thick snow, when he had seen a 14-year-old boy, shoeless and almost naked, begging from passers-by. The Superintendent had been so touched by the sight that, with colleagues at Old Trafford Police Station, he had collected for, and organised, a soup kitchen for hungry children. By the third night after its opening, 850 shivering children were queuing in the bitter cold.

No wonder that it was an age when drink, the great escape, was also the national curse. Each year 100,000 people were arrested for drunkenness, a quarter of them women.

Individual policemen might be kind in an era when want was everywhere, but the Law was not. The protection of property was strictly enforced. No-one, except for a few cranky reformers despised for their soft-heartedness, felt other than satisfaction when heavy prison sentences were awarded to wrongdoers, even first offenders. There was no public cry of protest when a mother of five children, with an invalid husband, who stole a pot of jam from the firm where she had been employed for fourteen years, was sent to prison for eighteen months.

The Law was quite a hobby with Mr. Thompson. His friends knew it was his wont to spend many hours in the Public Gallery at Bow Street Police Court, where, he said, the parade of human viciousness and folly passing through its dock was an object lesson in the wickedness of misguided men and women.

The men of substance—like Mr. Thompson—with solid golden sovereigns in their pockets, were a great deal more vexed and perturbed by the fact that Russia had recently mounted an imperial attack upon Turkey with the object of capturing Constantinople.

Public opinion had been inflamed by this Russian aggression and large crowds had stood outside the Houses of Parliament singing the popular ditty:

> "We don't want to fight but by jingo if we do
> "We've got the ships, we've got the men, we've got the money too.
> "We've fought the Bear before and while Britain shall be true
> "The Russians shall not have Constantinople".

Mr. Thompson had *not* taken the popular view. As a man of Faith he could not see, he told his friends, how a Christian country could support the heathen Turks against a nation of fellow Christians. "Violence is a failure of civilisation," he would add; "I take my stand as a Pacifist." His friends would smile a little indulgently. *They* rather enjoyed Britain's might, now deployed all over the world at little inconvenience to themselves. But then, they all knew Mr. Thompson had his little eccentricities. Not that they minded that. He was a capital fellow.

Mr. Thompson and his family were comparatively new to the district and at first there had been reservations. In Peckham in 1878 social delineations were firmly drawn—and strongly defended. To meet for the first time, Mr. Thompson was a striking, even bizarre figure. Small and lame, his almost white hair contrasted markedly with a dark brown face of simian cast. It was apparent that he tended to cultivate an excessive gentility of manner to conceal a somewhat rougher interior—not that anybody cared about this. Many were disguising a similarly humble origin, for whole new "middle" classes had sprung into being with the growing prosperity of Britain.

There were those—prompted no doubt by envy in an age when sanctity was a valuable status symbol—who said that Mr. Thompson's chief fault was a readiness to indulge in moral homily, almost at the drop of his own top hat.

This was not then, of course, the social crime it might be today. Peckham was a place for those who "had arrived." Most of its residents were retired shopkeepers and those who after years of devoted service in the City had attained Head Clerkships.

When they surveyed the reckless indigence of the teeming poor crammed into the reeking slums that haunted the nightmares of those poised socially just above them, they too permitted themselves to thank their Maker that they were not as other men. Mr. Thompson, after all, was "one of us". He was a regular attender at the local Anglican church and none spoke the "Amens" more fervently than he.

There was, too, something winning about him as he pottered about the district in his long black coat and top hat, pressing a halfpenny and a word of kindly exhortation upon those ragged children who happened to stray in from rougher areas. "I would do nothing to harm the poor," he told acquaintances. Not that he would encourage them to be uppity. In those days people knew their station, or their betters put them firmly into it. Snubbing presumptuous lower orders was almost a hobby; people exchanged over their tea-cups little stories of the cutting remarks they had made to those who had shown insufficient respect to rank. Deceived into folly by his genial manner, no doubt, a local milkman and a greengrocer had presumed to salute Mr. Thompson in altogether too comradely a way. He had put them firmly where they belonged with a reference to the undesirability of "low public-house *habitués*".

Mr. Thompson was no bigot, however. He frequently dropped into the Hollydale Tavern and other local "houses". He never himself took more than one drink, but he was generous in standing drinks to others. He could afford it, of course. He was known to be of excellent independent means. Nobody knew just how, but when he spoke of his "business interests" he spoke as one with no financial worries. Indeed he could be seen to live well and the pony and gig he drove about the neighbourhood made a smart turnout. He spent lavishly with the local tradesmen and they spoke warmly of him as a customer who paid "cash on the nail".

Mr. Thompson was respected for his commercial probity—always a virtue to endear a man to the more stable elements of society. But, above all else, he had one characteristic that was bound to recommend him to his fellow countrymen—a consuming love of animals. No. 5 East Terrace was over-run with his pets. It was more like a small menagerie. There were dogs, cats, pigeons, a parrot, a cockatoo—all trained to instant obedience at a word from their doting master.

To the majority of his neighbours Mr. Thompson was the epitome of amiable old bufferdom. But he was not idle. He and another local resident, Mr. Brion, were in touch with both the British and German Navies with regard to their joint invention to raise sunken vessels by pumping air into their hulls. Bevies of excited small boys had danced attendance upon them as the two grown men had gravely experimented with toy yachts at a local pond.

They had called at the Houses of Parliament to try to interest an M.P. in their invention. Many Peckhamites felt that they might yet have two famous men living among them.

There were those—the presumptuous milkman among them—who were unkind enough to say that there was something "rather rum" about Mr. Thompson; that he was in the habit of wearing different coloured wigs beneath that hard hat; that when not wearing gloves he was careful to keep his left hand concealed within the breast of his overcoat; that when strangers came down the street, he wore about him an air not altogether divorced from furtiveness.

There were even sharp-eyed and unkindly observers who said that Mr. Thompson was not always so resolutely genial as he appeared. In the ordinary course of events there are always occasions for little differences between people. A few, a very few, who had had occasion to vex Mr. Thompson, had been uncomfortably aware that at such times to look into the dark eyes hidden behind gold spectacles was rather like getting a glimpse into the furious depths of a blast furnace when the door is flung open—very smoky and scorching indeed.

Of course, he did have his trials. Mrs. Thompson, of the full figure and mass of rather unruly hair, was known to have a partiality for gin. One of the local wine merchants had shaken his head and murmured that something like £3 a week was going out of the house in drink.

Whenever Mrs. Thompson went out without her devoted husband Mrs. Ward was apt to go too—almost as though she was keeping an eye on her.

Mrs. Thompson had been seen on one occasion to sport a black eye. No-one thought too much of this. It was an age when wives were treated robustly. Among the lower orders, wife-beating was almost a weekend pastime. However, the Peckham-ites were inclined to feel that Mr. Thompson's domestic life was not quite as decorous as it might be. In fact, the truth of Mr. Thompson's matrimonial state was even more unusual than the most uncharitable Peckham-ite suspected. Mrs. Thompson was not "Mrs" Thompson at all. She was that pious gentleman's mistress, and the lodger, Mrs. Ward, was his legal spouse.

But the little household, as they made their music that evening, and drank a glass or two of stout and gin to sweeten their throats, made a snug tableau of Victorian decorum. For that evening at least tensions were eased in the pleasures of devotional music.

Mr. Thompson maintained, as was proper, a firm if kindly control over his dependents. When "Mrs." Thompson attempted to charge her glass of spirits a little more frequently than was seemly, she was immediately called to order by her master. A reproving wag of the forefinger and a "now, lass, now" sufficed to check any regrettable tendency to over-indulgence.

A last Moody and Sankey hymn was sung, occasioning Mr. Thompson to remark, as he did by habit, "Makes a man feel nearer 'is Maker to sing them lovely tunes." The ladies tidied up, while Mr. Thompson smoked a last pipe. By 10 p.m. the house was dark. "Early to bed, early to rise." Mr. Thompson was not, however, in bed.

Just after midnight the back door of the house opened slightly and Mr. Thompson, now wearing dark overcoat and a low brimmed hard hat slipped out and stood in the shadow of the house. He glanced up at the sky. There had been a slight fall of rain late in the evening, but it was dry now, with a strong wind blowing dark clouds across a bright hunter's moon.

A high railway embankment rose at the back of Mr. Thompson's home. It was the presence of this railway line that had led Mr. Thompson to choose this particular house as his dwelling. The noise of passing trains was a minor inconvenience beside the fact that it provided one useful social amenity—it enabled Mr. Thompson to enter and leave the house without putting curious neighbours to the worry of seeing him and wondering where he was going. At night he could walk along the track, dropping back into the streets at a convenient spot.

He climbed to the top and stood for a moment, watching and listening. In the moonlight from the line he had—as he still would have today—a wonderful panoramic view of London, from the heights of Hampstead Heath, across the silhouettes of the Houses of Parliament, east to St. Paul's and further east still the spider-web of cranes of Dockland.

In 1878 London was a darker city at night than it is today, and quieter. Outside the rip-roaring vice area of the West End, where "heavy swells", a legion of prostitutes and petty criminals jostled one another in the gin-palaces and "night houses", the streets were dark tunnels lit at infrequent intervals by street lamps. The only sounds were the steady tramp of stray pedestrians and the clip-clop of a horse-drawn cab or private carriage. By midnight all was still, most of the houses dark and the streets empty.

Glancing quickly round, Mr. Thompson began to walk at a rapid pace along the railway track to the east.

Police Constable R202 Edward Robinson was keeping an alert look-out as he made for his 2 a.m. rendezvous with his Sergeant. South London, indeed the whole of southern England, had been plagued by an epidemic of burglaries, carried out persistently over many months. Detectives believed the robberies to be the work of one highly skilled craftsman, but all efforts to catch him had been unavailing. Normally the police concentrated on the centre of cities and left the suburbs to infrequent foot constable patrols, but now special patrols had been mounted in the richer residential districts of the Metropolis. In Blackheath, for example, a district of "gentlemen's" houses, the raids had been so frequent that Lord Truro had drawn attention to them in the House of Lords. "What were the police doing?" he had asked.

Constable Robinson was, therefore, keeping his eyes very wide open as he walked his beat along the avenue leading from St. John's Park to Blackheath. A mansion-style house owned by wealthy Mr. J. A. Burness stood in its own grounds to his left. He glanced at its dark bulk, and as he did so a small flicker of

The last photograph taken of Charles Peace

By courtesy of The Sheffield Star

Charles Peace on trial

From a sketch by Frank Lockwood

Peace, wrapped in blankets after throwing himself from a train to avoid sentence, is confronted by Mrs. Dyson

light flared for a second behind a downstairs window. Robinson checked his steady pace and waited. Like most London policemen of his day he was large and imperturbable. The house was dark again. A few moments later there was another flicker of light—again instantly quenched—in an upstairs room.

Robinson thought quickly, but calmly. The house was a large one with many exits. This was a job for more than one man. He walked on to his checkpoint with Police Constable R284 William Girling. Girling was waiting in the shadows.

"Come on."

The two men went back to Mr. Burness's house, Robinson describing in a few short sentences what he had seen. Back at the rear of the house the two men watched. Again there was a glimmer of light from an upstairs window. "Up you go," whispered Girling. He helped Robinson climb on to the garden wall. At this moment Police Sergeant R32 Charles Brown appeared along the avenue, and there was a hurried conference. The Sergeant helped Girling on to the wall beside Robinson. Then he made his way round to the front garden. The two policemen crouching on the wall heard the sound of the front door bell clang through the house.

It must have been a heart-stopping clamour to the man creeping stealthily from room to room. He was not, however, a man to be paralysed by his fright. Within seconds a window on the ground floor was flung up, a dark figure tumbled out and raced down the garden path towards the back wall.

Robinson dropped off the wall into the garden and ran towards the fleeing burglar. Girling jumped down into the road and ran to head him off. The quarry doubled in his tracks with the speed of a turning hare. Robinson pounded after him through the garden and began to gain steadily.

The prowler stopped and wheeled round. The moon broke through the clouds and, stark in its brilliant light, Robinson saw a seamed face, distorted with hate, gazing at him along the barrel of a revolver. "Keep off, keep back, or, by God, I'll shoot you."

"You had better not." Robinson moved forward relentlessly.

The revolver flashed twice, the first shot going to the right of the policeman's head, the second to the left as the gunman tried to correct his aim.

Robinson let his momentum carry him on. It was an act of tremendous courage and he must surely have died, but for a lucky accident. He slipped on the wet grass and fell backwards as the third bullet slammed through the air where his head had been a second before. He scrambled to his feet and dodged behind a tree. Again the pistol roared. Robinson sprang out from his cover, striking with all his power at the ferocious mask of a face as the gunman sought to aim for a killing shot. There was a snarl of rage. "You bugger, I'll settle you this time." A fifth shot was fired and the bullet tore through Robinson's right arm as he instinctively threw it up to protect his head.

He flung himself on his assailant and bore the writhing figure to the ground, seizing the pistol arm with one hand, squeezing the throat with the other. The body beneath him went limp. A whining voice pleaded: "Let me up. I'll go quietly." Robinson could see that, even as he spoke, the man was trying to pluck a knife from an inside pocket of his coat. The Constable doubled up the man's arm, grabbed the pistol—which was strapped to the wrist—and struck his prisoner several blows on the head with his own weapon. With a groan the man went limp. Weakening rapidly through loss of blood, Robinson rolled the man over on his face and pinioned him with knee and uninjured arm.

Sergeant Brown came running round the side of the house. He struck with his truncheon at the outflung pistol hand, then wrenched the pistol away. Girling was hard on his heels. The two men dragged the battered raider to his feet, and he stood silent as they went through his pockets, fishing out a small jemmy and a battery of small tools.

Girling told Robinson: "I've got him. Better get down to the Station and get your arm dressed." Robinson dragged himself to his feet and began to stumble away for help, and the burglar remarked, with a distinct note of righteous indignation in his voice: "I only did it to frighten him so that I could get away." He seemed to feel that this answered all possible accusations against his conduct.

"Come on you."

Girling made to march the prisoner away. They had only gone a few paces when a change of step forced the Constable to shift his grip on the seemingly dejected figure. The limp form came alive and made a desperate attempt to twist away into the darkness. The only reward was a series of blows from Girling's truncheon.

Sergeant Brown had now been let into the house by the occupants, who had been woken by the shots. He found on the dining-room table silverware and other valuables piled in a neat heap ready for packing and removal. He saw that the burglar had jemmied his way in through one of the windows of a room at the rear of the house. The door leading out into the hall had been locked for the night, so the intruder had cut a neat hole, five inches square, in one panel to enable him to put his hand through and turn the key. He had been coolly surveying the upstairs rooms when alarmed by Brown ringing the door bell. Altogether the place showed the handiwork of an exceptionally skilled professional housebreaker.

Girling, aided by other officers who had come up, frog-marched the man to Greenwich Police Station, where he was charged with burglary and the attempted murder of P.C. Robinson. He seemed subdued, but when asked his name spat "Find out". The police entered in the charge book: "Man, name and age refused. Complexion dark, clean shaven, hair grey, eyes hazel, one darker than the other, large mouth, long scar on side of left leg and back of thigh. Forefinger of left hand deficient."

The prisoner was then locked in a cell. He seemed in a bad way, moaning and groaning. A kindly constable passed him some hard-boiled eggs through the grating. "Oh, would to God, Sergeant," came the piteous lament, "you would come in here and knock my brains out, I feel so bad."

He kept up a stream of complaint as he tried to eat the eggs despite the pain of his battered face, every sentence prefixed or punctuated with such expressions as "Oh, My God", or "May God forgive me."

"He was a real canting old rogue," an inspector commented later.

However, after eating his eggs, the elderly felon lay down on his board and slept peacefully until wakened for his breakfast later the same morning. He was taken before the magistrates and remanded in custody for a week. A local newspaper said of him that he was "of negro type with face bandaged."

There was no doubt he had been damaged in the struggle. One could hardly expect otherwise. The police would have been saints not to have dealt hardly with a man who had made so determined an effort to kill one of their comrades. The prisoner seems to have accepted rough handling as a hazard of his calling, though he did subsequently complain: "I should not have cared if they had not kicked me, but they did and hurt me severely as I am suffering from fistula." He spoke with an air of moral superiority, as one who knew himself to be blameless in life's rough and tumble.

On October 18th he again appeared before the Greenwich Magistrates and was once more remanded in custody for a week. This time he gave his name as John Ward and his age as 60. He seemed eager to be accepted as a rather feeble old man, more to be pitied than otherwise. The police, however, had seen his agility on the night of his arrest and were not surprised to note that when stripped his body was that of a much younger man, indeed an unusually muscular and active man; though, when dressed and in public, his frame seemed to shrink into elderly decrepitude.

There was some evidence offered at his second court appearance. It was stated that the knife found in his possession had belonged to a Dulwich shipbuilder whose home had been burgled a year before. The "aged" Mr. Ward was obviously a man careful with possessions—once they had come into his own grasp.

In addition to this commendable display of thrift, Mr. Ward exhibited other qualities of the kind inculcated in Victorian moral tales. He was certainly not afraid to speak up as a champion of truth, even at the risk of personal unpopularity. In the police wagon on his way to Newgate Prison, where he was to stay on remand, he did not fear, despite the roughness of his travelling companions, to issue a strong rebuke to a young man who had landed in trouble through drink; nor did he allow himself to be deterred from his high moral purpose by the shouts and curses of his fellow prisoners. He maintained his stand until a policeman told him: "Shut up, you old humbug." Then he subsided into an injured silence.

The authorities were aware that they had a highly experienced criminal in their grasp. For one thing the number of burglaries in the Metropolis fell off. But the problem was to establish Mr. Ward's real identity. The fingerprint system was as yet unknown, criminal records were in their infancy, and Mr. Ward did not show any eagerness to assist them. The Chief Warders were summoned from other prisons to see if they could recognise him. "You've never seen me before," he told them indignantly, "I've never been in a place like this before." This statement was contradicted by his intimate knowledge of prison routine and his insistence on any privileges allowed to a prisoner on remand.

He seemed, moreover, to be quite at home. He invented a little game with his captors which afforded him great amusement. He would stick his head out of his cell, through the old-fashioned grille door. "Hey, young fellow," he would call to a warder on duty, "take a good look." He would pop his head back in again. A moment later the astonished warder would see a quite different face emerge, every feature twisted and contorted out of recognition; the jaw pushed out of shape; the eyebrows disappearing up into the scalp; the whole writhing in a pantomime of expression that would not have disgraced a malevolent chimpanzee. The look of amazement on the spectator's face would evoke a burst of cackling laughter from Mr. Ward. "There, would you swear to me then? As an honest man now, could you?" It was noticeable, too, that as the days went by, Mr. Ward's dark brown skin began to become perceptibly lighter, as though some staining was fading. His "negroid" appearance obviously was of cosmetic origin.

Police Constable Robinson called to see him and Mr. Ward expressed great satisfaction to learn that the wound in his arm had healed. He wished the gallant constable well, though making it quite clear that to avoid capture he would have "done for him" without remorse.

By November however Mr. Ward's protective shell of self-satisfaction was beginning to wear thin. Mental pressures of loneliness began to operate.

Mr. Brion, the Peckham inventor, was bewildered to receive on November 1st the following letter addressed from Newgate Prison.

"My Dear Sir Mr. Brion,

I do not know how to write to you or what to say for my heart is near broken for I am nearly mad to think I have got into this fearful mess, all with giving myself up to drinking. Oh Mr. Brion do you have pity on me. Do not despise me as my family has done for I do not know ware they are for they have broken up there home and gon I do not know ware.

So O my dear sir I must beg you to have mercy upon me and come to see me.

Your reckard
john ward

You can come heney week day from one till two o'clock and inquire for John Ward for trial."

Curiosity took Mr. Brion post-haste to Newgate. He was astonished when into the visitors' room shuffled Mr. Thompson, the pacifist, whose absence from East Terrace had caused some comment in the neighbourhood. He was thought to be "away on holiday", though the more knowing in the district had expressed the belief that Mr. Thompson had finally had enough of Mrs. Thompson's drinking.

Subsequently there had been rumours that the house was quite empty and that Mrs. Thompson, in tears, had taken refuge with friends in the district.

Mr. Brion was not able to answer his friend's eager questions about the whereabouts of his family. He was, in fact, too bemused by surprise to take in much of what was being said. He left his former colleague as soon as he decently could and hastened to the police to tell them his story.

A large force of detectives descended on 5, East Terrace. Inside they found an Aladdin's cave of booty from scores of robberies all over London, and an arsenal of burglar's tools and firearms. Ransacking Mr. Thompson's workshop they discovered, in addition to plans and models for various ingenious inventions, equipment for the melting down of gold and silverware. But of the other members of the happy family there was no trace.

The detectives set out on the trail. Mrs. Ward and Willie, they were told, had left the day after Mr. Thompson's disappearance, bearing a large number of boxes. It seemed that despite being closely guarded and seemingly badly hurt Mr. Thompson had somehow managed to convey a message from Greenwich Police Station to his home: a mystery which was to puzzle and irritate the police for some time.

They did not however find it difficult to trace Mrs. Thompson, who was obviously not as adept as her companions in the art of social mobility. She was found to be staying locally and the police called upon her. There were many things they wanted to know and, as is their way, they were prepared to allow a small fish to escape if it aided in netting a larger. They spoke to Mrs. Thompson in tones both conciliatory and menacing. Did she realise she was in trouble? Might she not be sensible and perhaps make amends at this late stage? Under certain circumstances her part in these matters could be overlooked if—. It was all too much for Mrs. Thompson who, since she had lost the stabilising influence of her lord and master, had been taking to her favourite gin with ever-increasing abandon. The pious Mr. Thompson's suburban paradise was to prove that it had harboured that amenity common to so many paradises of man's devising—the delightful but unreliable presence of an Eve. Mrs. Thompson took up residence with the Brions and thought things over. She took a few more drinks and reached certain conclusions.

She asked if she might see Police Inspectors Bonney and Philips, the officers in charge of the case against Mr. Ward, or Thompson. They appeared post-haste in Mr. Brion's drawing-room. Standing nervously, her hands twisting, Mrs. Thompson murmured references to a possible reward. Did the police realise that Mr. Thompson was also Mr. Charles Peace, late of Sheffield, Yorkshire, who had himself made jocular references to "they would give £100 for me there"?

The two police inspectors looked at one another for a moment. Indeed "they" would give £100 for Mr. Peace in Sheffield. It was a reward that had been on offer in every police station in the country for many a long month. They had not bargained for as big a capture as this.

An old fox had run his last race.

Charles Frederick Peace. Wanted for over two years for the murder of a neighbour whose wife had had the misfortune to rouse Peace's always red-hot sexual ardour; who had left a trail of crime all over the country, despite the fact that his striking appearance was known to every police office; who had openly sneered that no detective was clever enough to catch him.

Peace, the thief, whose skill and audacity had led to his nickname "The King" among his own kind; the burglar whose long record in the files bore the warning "Always goes armed, will shoot."

Today, eighty years after that night in a Blackheath garden when P.C. Robinson's courage finally wrote finis to a one-man crime wave, Peace is still remembered as a sort of folk legend by many who never saw him, were not born when he died, and have only the vaguest conception of his life story. Within weeks of his death he became a myth. Thousands in the great industrial towns who had never read a word about him knew exactly who "Charlie Peace" was and something of his legend. Sherlock Holmes was the 'tec. Charlie Peace was the crook. This is still true in parts of the industrial north and among many Cockney Londoners.

An air-raid warden in Peckham entered a shelter one night in March 1941 when the German bombers were overhead and told his friends: "They've got old Charlie's house tonight." His audience knew he meant that the famous local landmark—5 East Terrace—had been hit.

Peace was the last of those bloody ruffians, like Dick Turpin, Jack Sheppard, and perhaps even Robin Hood, who have become dear to the Anglo-Saxon heart. It is possible that deep in the English subconscious there is a vein of repressed larceny; perhaps it is that there is a dim racial memory, dating back to the Norman Conquest, when the outlaw was often the man who defied and plundered the hated authority—the dreaded overlord. It may be that it is an ancient zest for anarchy in a nation known, until Victorian times when a wave of puritanism swept the country, for its turbulence, capacity for riot and brutality. Perhaps from the same depths of mixed emotions springs the fact that even now, in the socially progressive England of today, the Hangman remains one of the most popular public entertainers, a creature of dreaded fascination.

The popular image of Peace was blurred and adapted to

his time, even as that of earlier heroes in the same genre was adapted to theirs. In an older pastoral England, Dick Turpin, the highwayman who rode Black Bess to York, was looked upon as a gay blade who robbed the vaunting rich as they rode in carriages along the roads where poorer and maybe more honest men walked in the mud. In reality Turpin was a despicable footpad, a coward who terrorised the poor and unprotected, killed in cold blood and who would have been incapable of riding Black Bess to York—even had he owned a horse called Black Bess.

What is the truth of Peace? Was he a sort of Raffles, a thief of social conscience, honour and wit as many believe? Why did many who had known him speak of him in later years with a sort of wry affection? Was he the Yorkshire "caution"—the man of hard-headed drollery the word suggests?

Stories of him are legion. They paint the picture of a likeable villain, plundering the homes of the wealthy manufacturers who had made their gold from the work of underfed masses crowded into evil slums; a man generous to the distressed, who combined theft with Christianity, doing good works and teaching in Sunday Schools; a master of disguise almost literally tweaking the noses of the police; a great musician, a peaceful home-loving husband and father, who was also the irresistible lover of scores of women; a rogue who liked a jest as well as a purse.

Many of the things legend says of him are true, or almost so. He did perform many of the feats attributed to him. He was, alas, no Raffles; he was more interesting than that. In many ways he was a monster of criminality, almost the prototype law-breaker—utterly egotistical, rapacious, prepared to kill for a desire or to escape capture, but he was a man with identifiable human emotions and motives common to everybody. He was brave, he was affectionate, he was clever. He undoubtedly possessed artistic gifts.

Peace was a grotesque, but also a truly representative Victorian figure. Society, after all, gets the criminals it deserves. Even his enemies, the police, spoke of him with something akin to admiration. He was an original. The mould was broken after the fates had created "Charlie Peace".

In his own time huge crowds flocked to see him and during

his last trial reporters filed 180,000 words through the local telegraph office to keep abreast with the public interest. When a photograph was displayed in a shop in Regent Street, a reporter wrote, "The footpath of this part of the finest street in Europe was for hours together simply impassable as Peers of the Realm, beautiful women, politicians, rogues, soldiers, pickpockets and policemen all jostled one another together in their eagerness to catch a glimpse of the picture of this supreme rascal."

Madame Tussauds, the famous London waxworks museum, commissioned an artist in wax to prepare two effigies of Peace and they stand to this day in the famous Chamber of Horrors.

Part of Peace's fascination was in himself, part in his deeds. It is difficult to comprehend a man who can express simple fervour and belief in God and yet who can watch a young man sentenced to death for a murder he had himself committed. There were those who said that Peace's God was the Devil, but he himself had no theological confusion of identity. He said simply "I believe in God. I believe in the Devil. I fear neither."

"Charlie Peace" was both the first and the last of his type. He was the first great criminal of the huge towns that sprang into existence after the Industrial Revolution. He spanned Victorian England. When he was born—almost up to the time when he picked his first pocket—Britain had no organised police force. Men were still transported for petty theft. He died as the highly organised efficient police systems of today were coming into existence. If he had not lived it would have been necessary for a great novelist to invent him, though even Dickens might have hesitated to portray such a character. He was the quintessence of the "Old Lags", the illiterate brutes who sprang from the awful slums of the new manufacturing towns with only cunning and brute ferocity to help them in their raids on a rich and repressive society. They have gone now, replaced by the modern machine-tooled mobsters as highly skilled as the Technical Age they prey on.

Peace was a lone wolf, with cunning elevated to genius and with a capacity for unctuous hypocrisy bordering on the farcical, but he was of his time. "One of us" against "them" to thousands of harshly driven Victorian poor, who, huddled in the mean streets, ill-housed, ill-used and neglected by society from the cradle to the grave, forgot his crimes and remembered only his cheeky defiance of authority. Even now there are echoes of that world of gaslight and squalor in the shrill voices of the children, who, playing in the streets, still sing as a skipping rope chant:—

"I love Charlie
Charlie was a thief
Charlie killed a copper
Charlie came to grief
Charlie came to our house
Stole some bread and jam
Eat my mother's pudden
Eat my father's ham
When the coppers caught him
They hung him on a rope
Poor old Charlie
You haven't got a hope."

CHAPTER TWO

PEACE WAS born in an England in transition. It still retained something of the old rural economy when most men earned their living from the land and were content with their station in small, tight-knit communities, but these traditional social patterns were being swept aside as the great new towns attracted more and more people to work in the new industries. In these towns, in conditions of appalling overcrowding with poverty for the many and opulence for the few, was created the wealth that enabled the country to acquire its vast empire.

It was a time of opportunity, especially for the clever and ruthless who were prepared to exploit the drudgery of others to their own ends. It was a process that destroyed many of the simpler folk who found a village standard of living did not equip them to cope with the *furore* of the new towns. Christopher Mayhew, the Quaker reformer and social historian, wrote, "There is a tone of morality throughout the rural districts of England, which is unhappily wanting in the large towns and centres of manufacture. Commerce is incontestably demoralising."

"Charlie" Peace was born on May 14th, 1832, in Angel Court, Nursery Street, then a poverty-stricken area in Sheffield, in the West Riding of Yorkshire. Sheffield was one of the greatest of the new industrial towns which, throughout the North and Midlands, had spread like a dark stain over the landscape.

In modern Britain it is almost impossible to visualize the horrors of the poorer quarters of these towns. Housing was of the poorest quality, flung up anywhere by small builders and speculators. Many dwellings were without ventilation or drainage. They sprawled among the factory chimneys, under a greasy pall of smoke. Sewage was non-existent and the stench was overwhelming. There were no parks, no trees, no amenities —except the gin shops and public houses. Hordes of ragged men, women and children, living on subsistence wages, racked by disease, often lousy, swarmed in the filthy streets and crowded into the mean houses to live—and to die in enormous numbers. Not surprisingly the pubs and gin palaces did roaring trade night and day. They were the only places in which solace could be found, for drink was cheap and potent.

On the outskirts of these towns lived the rich, getting steadily richer. They looked down on the swarming humanity in the towns in much the same way as the early colonists overseas looked down on the natives—as a different and rather dangerous species. Instinctively they drew away, putting up a social barrier between themselves and the misery-created vice and degradation of the masses.

Peace was the youngest of three surviving children in his family. It was typical of the times that his mother and his father came from different places and, more important, somewhat different social classes. At the time of his birth the family was poor, living on the meagre proceeds of a small shoemaker's shop.

The father, John Peace, was then in his late forties, somewhat elderly to be the father of young children. He had begun life as a collier in Burton-on-Trent, which suggests the humblest of origins, for the men—and women—who worked underground then were treated little better than beasts of burden. The mines themselves were ill-lit, badly ventilated holes and tunnels in the ground; safety precautions were unknown and casualties and fatalities frequent and little heeded. John Peace, like his son Charlie, was to be a victim of the reckless indifference to human life and suffering shown by the leaders of the new Industrial Age. He lost a leg and had to leave the pits.

He was a man of great strength of character and determination. Despite his handicap he became a trainer of wild animals and for many years worked with a travelling show, giving performances with his trained lions and tigers. One of his specialities was arranging fights between lions and packs of bulldogs—a bloody spectacle of slaughter that thrilled the rough audiences with delight. He prospered and bought a financial interest in the show.

It was at a fair at Rotherham that the wild animal trainer—a widower with a small son to bring up—met a young woman of rather higher social status, the daughter of a surgeon in the Royal Navy. It was she who was to become the mother of Charlie Peace. She was many years younger than John Peace—she was to survive him by nearly half a century—but, despite his disability, his grizzled good looks and the authority of his character attracted her. Perhaps, too, she was dazzled by the freedom and excitement of his roving life. They had a quick courtship, were married at Rotherham Church and set out on their travels with the show.

Another son, Willie, was born and as soon as he could walk the resourceful father saw in him an added attraction to the show. Nightly, Willie accompanied him into his cage of wild beasts to the applause of the audiences. John Peace must have been very sure of his control over the animals for both he and his wife doted on Willie. Their world was temporarily shattered when he caught the dreaded smallpox, then endemic in Britain, and died within a few days. Charlie Peace was to say later, "after that my father could not bear to be with the beasts."

John Peace sold out to his business associates and left the show. He never afterwards tamed an animal, but he passed on much of his skill and knowledge to his youngest child. For a time the old nomadic life went on, for John invested his money in swings and roundabouts and travelled the Fairs. But he was getting on and hankered after a settled life, so the family settled down in Sheffield. He was a jack of all trades and started a shoemaking shop, but it did not prosper. The house in Nursery Street where Charlie was born was a mean affair, built with its door below pavement level.

A daughter, Mary Ann, had been born about two years before; she was to be Charlie's favourite and, indeed, was to be involved in his earliest "scrapes". Another brother, Dan, was to survive Charlie. The family was affectionate within its own confines and all his life Charlie had strong family loyalties.

Charlie Peace's family background would yield many clues to a psychologist about why he became the man he did. He had an ageing father, and the children of an aged parent are often exceptional. From his father, too, he inherited a taste for a wandering life, for movement for its own sake, a great skill with animals and a capacity to turn his hand to many trades.

Mrs. Peace is an enigmatic figure. Little is known of her, except that she was devoted to Charlie and he to her. At least once he risked his liberty and his life to visit her. The most that reports say of her is that she was a "doubtful" character and a "bit of a cadger".

Her effect on him in childhood may have been decisive. Born into a higher social class she found herself, during Charlie's childhood, reduced to poverty in conditions that were a torment to the hardiest. Might it not be that she poured into the ears of the infant on her knee the complaint that she—and he—were designed for better things, to be by rights members of those classes taking their ease in the opulent houses outside the town.

Charlie was fond of his parents, but from the beginning was an unruly child. He would recount when grown-up how, when he could not master his mother any other way, he would tie her in her chair and then tease her. It must have been a formidable child who would resist the iron will of a former wild animal trainer, but perhaps the father rather admired the waywardness and force of character of his youngest and did not check him.

Certainly John Peace was not a spent force. He gave up his shop and became a coal dealer and carter; the family moved to Stanley Street in the Wicker district and subsequently to Water Lane, when John took up his last enterprise, the running of a public-house.

Young Charlie was sent to two schools, Pitsmoore School and Hebblethwaite's in Paradise Square. He was a poor scholar and always admitted, "I did not take kindly to book learning, preferring to spend my time 'knacking' about odd jobs, anything where ingenuity was displayed or which brought me into connection with animals."

His first battles with authority were in school and he seems to have got his own way, though in those days children were not handled with the kindness they are today. Blows and terror were considered the legitimate means of forcing knowledge into children.

In only one place was he consistently well behaved—his Sunday School. His teacher there was to say in later years that he was "a well-behaved lad".

Altogether he was a strange hobgoblin of a child, a mixture

of magpie and monkey. He was adept at all sorts of pursuits and hobbies. He was fond of cutting figures from paper—an entertainment he was to pursue in prison—and once cut out from one piece of paper a whole stag hunt, with horses, dogs, gates, trees and a stag. He also had a cat, of which he was fond, and he trained her to perform many tricks. He built her a set of harness and a little cart to pull along. He also built a peepshow under a table and invited his playmates in and put on performances of melodramas.

As he got older he added other tricks of skill and strength to his repertoire, making a leather socket in the shape of a cup which he fastened to his forehead. He would then throw up a heavy shot and catch it in the cup.

Towards the end of his life there were stories that even at school he was a thief, robbing his playmates, but Charlie always denied this and when his earlier acquaintances were asked to substantiate these charges by instances, could only refer lamely to an expedition to "scrump" apples from an orchard.

He was said, too, to have been a merciless street fighter and bully. He undoubtedly was a wiry little scrapper, but then a boy had to be, living in those districts in those years. It was a rough age, when men brawled, especially when drunk, and the youngsters followed suit. Grown men would put two boys to "a mill" for their amusement, sometimes feeding them heavy quantities of ale to stupefy them against punishment and, therefore, able to fight the more ferociously.

For the era, Charlie's was not an unhappy childhood. The family had a home and ate regularly, which was more than did thousands of others. The Peace family kept afloat through the political and social discontent, born of desperation, which erupted when Charlie was ten. There was a general cut in wages and rioting broke out on a large scale all over the country. There were many deaths as the mobs battled with militia and troops. In Manchester crowds of hungry workmen roamed the streets demanding money and food from the more prosperous pedestrians and offering violence if they were not accommodated. The upper and middle classes retreated into their houses, covering ground-floor windows with iron bars and bolting and padlocking heavy doors.

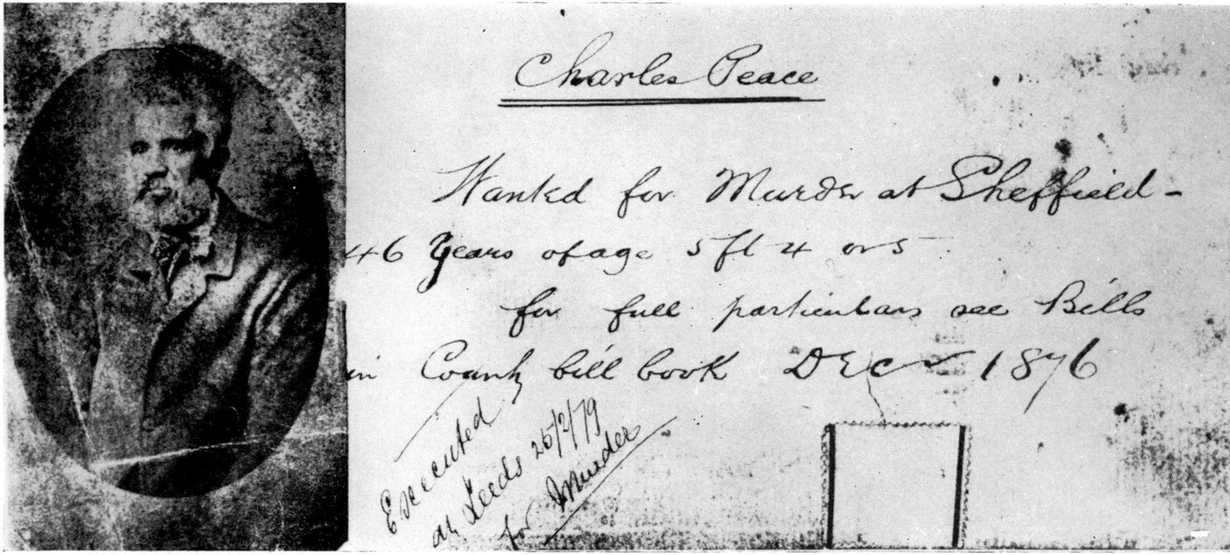
Charles Peace

Wanted for Murder at Sheffield –
46 Years of age 5 ft 4 or 5 –
for full particulars see Bills
in County bill book Dec 1876

Executed
at Leeds 25/2/79
for Murder

Extract from "Thieves' Album" of Manchester City Police

By courtesy of Manchester City Police

Description of No. 9170 George Parker 55 Released
on Ticket of Leave from Millbank Prison,
on the 20th June 1864

Date and Place of Committal	9th June 1859 Salford
Date and Place of Conviction	10th Aug 1859 Liverpool
Crime	Receiving Stolen Goods
Sentence	6 Years P.S.
Trade or Occupation	Joiner
Complexion	Dark
Hair	Dark
Eyes	Brown
Height	5 feet 3½ inches
Marks	
Period of Sentence Unexpired	13 Months

Date of each Report.

DATE	RESIDENCE OF CONVICT	NAME, TRADE, AND ADDRESS, OF EMPLOYER
[illegible]	1 Court Orchard Street	
Oct 5	44 Kenyon Alley	In business for himself
Nov 1	Same	Same
Dec 6	Same	Same
Jany 3	Same	Same
Feb 1	Same	Same
Mar 1	Same	Same
Apr 4	Same	Same
May 2	Same	Same
June 1	Same	Same
July 4	Same	Same
Aug 2	Same	Same

Murder Committed 29th Nov 1876.
[illegible]

Hanged at Armley Gaol for the Murder of Mr. Dyson

Extract from "Ticket of Leave" book of Sheffield City Police

By courtesy of Sheffield City Police

Every town had its mob. To control it the millowners and shopkeepers enrolled in the militia, or the special constabulary. Detachments of troops were sent north—where the trouble was naturally at its worst—and the insurrection crumbled. But it was a near thing. The poor turned back once more to the consolations of gin, or the fervours of evangelical religions promising a paradise hereafter. Throughout the early years of the century the great preachers of Methodism and the Nonconformist sects had had tremendous success among the labouring classes. It has been said, not without some truth, that Wesleyanism may well have saved England from a revolution.

It was in this atmosphere of unrest that Charlie grew up. It was the beginning of his own love-hate relationship with the wealthier classes, with the respectability and comfort of the stolid middle classes. One part of him drove him on to loot these harsh overlords, another—no doubt fostered by his mother—made him yearn to join them, to himself present a sedate front to the world.

John Peace had become a convert to the new wave of Christianity and Charlie accompanied him to meetings where religious feelings were whipped up to almost orgiastic heights. Perhaps something of the skilled, if unconscious, showmanship of the great preachers appealed to Charlie's instinctive love of the dramatic.

Because his father was now earning a fair living Charlie was spared the horrors of being driven out to work at eight or nine. He was twelve before he became an apprentice tinsmith, later switching over to the steel trade.

It was not a tempting future, though things had improved a little during the previous few years. In 1833 Lord Hokley, the Tory reformer, had tried to get working hours for children in mills and factories reduced to ten hours a day. He had met with stiff opposition; such a thing would ruin the economy, he was told. They had said that, of course, about the proposed abolition of the Slave Trade. At that time children of six or seven worked in the mills and were sometimes flogged to increase output. After all, the practical men of affairs argued, this was not inhumane, for sleepy children might doze off and drop into the machines. And, of course, to spend money on safety devices would ruin the economy.

By the time Charlie Peace began work the *régime* benevolently permitted children to work only six-and-a-half hours a day, six days a week. He was not, however, fated to remain a drudge of the industrial machine for very long. On the morning of his 14th birthday he was to be crippled for life.

He was working at Millsands Rolling Mills and the owner, called Mellard, had ordered him to help another boy who was behind with his work. Charlie turned to help his mate and a piece of red hot steel being rolled through his own machine went into the back of his left leg just above the knee and came out below the knee in front. There was only one way to get it out. Charlie was held tight and his machine was reversed, pulling the metal back out of his leg. He was then carried to a chemist's shop for first aid and then on a litter, unconscious, to Sheffield Infirmary. He did not emerge again for 18 months.

Hospitals were dreadful places then, badly run with inferior staffs and primitive brutal treatments. Death raced up and down the airless wards and corridors in the stink of corruption and dirt, for nothing was yet known about bacteria. Surgeons wore their old bloodstained coats to operate. Old bandages were re-used for economy. Charlie nonetheless survived an operation, performed, of course, without anaesthetics, for the removal of the shattered kneebone. Eventually he was discharged on crutches as incurable.

There was no such thing as compensation available to ease the wound socially. If a man got in the way of the machinery that was just too bad for the man. The psychological scars of Charlie's wound may have been deeper than the deep scars he was to bear on his leg for ever. Years later, looking back on a lifetime of crime, Peace said of this time, "When I at last did get better I had been so long idle I did not like to work". It was an excuse of reckless frivolity, lightly said perhaps to cover a bitterness too strong to be spoken of.

The tendons of the leg were damaged beyond repair and from then on the leg was apt to contract, making Peace walk on tiptoe. It is a measure of his inherent determination that he learned to walk in such a way as to disguise this infirmity and he grew up to be a man of great agility—indeed on occasions he actually earned money as an acrobat and tumbler.

Then to this adolescent, whose turbulent psyche had already

been disturbed by a disablement, came another blow. John Peace died on November 18th, 1848 at the age of 64.

The family put on the In Memoriam cards:—

"In Peace he lived.
In Peace he Died,
Life was our Desire
But God Denied".

It is said that the words were composed by Charles, but there is no proof of this, though he was always fond of expressing himself in writing, even if in a grammar and style of spelling of his own. There can be no doubt that it was a grievous loss to him for he had been fond of his father. But worse, without the strong hand of the former wild animal trainer to guide them, the family began to drift downwards.

Young Charlie Peace was not yet committed to outlawry when his father died. He was still working, at least part of the time, in Quaker Smith's steelyard in the Wicker, but other influences were about to be brought to bear to complete the final moulding of a character already embittered by suffering and the cruelties of society. He had always been fond of music and he began to learn the violin from a man named Joe Bethley, a watchmaker, in Division Street, Sheffield. Bethley was well known in the city and district as a musician, playing in public houses, gin palaces, and at local fairs and feasts. He played a big role in the Peace family history for Charlie's favourite sister, Mary Ann, lived with him for some years and bore him three children.

She may well have met him through her brother, for she was married previously to a man called Neil, a file-cutter by trade and a drunkard, dog-breeder and wife-beater by inclination. Throughout his early life Charlie was a sinewy and hard-hitting fist fighter. He thrashed Neil several times for ill-treating Mary Ann. Once, in revenge, Neil set his pet dog, a bulldog bitch notorious for her ferocity at the dog fights so popular among the steelworkers, to attack Charlie. The dog sprang at Charlie, but with great dexterity he leapt to one side, seized the animal by its lower jaw and beat it into unconsciousness with his other fist. He said afterwards, "The dog which never owned a master before, found one in me. She was so completely cowed that she would not face me again. I was the only living thing of whom she was afraid".

Despite his wiry toughness Charlie had great delicacy of touch with the violin and soon learned to play the instrument well. In fact, he learned to play a variety of musical instruments and became a touring musician in Sheffield, at first with Bethley, later on his own. It was in the "pubs" and low quarters of the city that he began to gravitate towards the worst elements, associating with the thieves and harlots who infested certain districts. He had already begun to steal whenever the chance presented itself—"I was a thief from the time I was 14", he said later—and he now began to learn the trade from his new friends.

His first criminal trade was picking pockets, now a dying art, but a prevalent form of crime in those days. Perhaps he came under the eye of a "kidsman", as thieves' argot dubbed men who made their living training children and youths to crime. He would have been taught to practise upon a figure that was covered with bells to vibrate at the slightest touch. The figure would be hung up and the novice would pick its pockets until such time as he could do so without making a single bell give tongue in warning.

Peace became a full-time itinerant musician, picking pockets as a profitable sideline, and even working honestly from time to time when things were slack. We know that one of his favourite ways of stealing was to fall, shamming illness, at the feet of a prospective victim, picking the man's pockets while being assisted to his feet. He did not despise women's purses. He was known on one occasion to have concealed himself in a booth in the women's lavatory at a Fair in Sheffield. He was in there most of the day, awaiting a chance to slip away, and afterwards recounted with great glee all he had heard and seen to his cronies in the stews and dramshops of the slums.

He was becoming a well-known figure in the city's tight knit underworld. In those days, and indeed until quite recently, criminals tended to huddle together to live, secluded from the society on which they preyed. It was highly dangerous for a stranger to penetrate into these closely guarded communities. Within them, amid the squalor of indigent living, drunkenness, promiscuity and violence, lived the burglars, pickpockets, footpads and hardened prostitutes, speaking their own argot and maintaining their own social structure in which force and cunning were the hallmarks of a good standing.

Each street within these jungles had its own "pub" in which every man or woman present was a thief, or worse. They presented a Hogarthian scene, brutish and cunning faces, sodden with drunkenness, seamed with every human vice, quarrelling, laughing or whispering in the gloom of low-turned lamps and swirling tobacco smoke. The very air trembled with repressed violence on the part of the men and scarcely repressed hysteria on the part of the women. Often there would be a pandemonium of screams and curses as a drunken woman would fling herself on a rival in a whirlwind of scratching and biting, or men would battle with fists, teeth and boots. No mercy was shown to man, or woman, when once "downed". That was the time for the crippling kick or blow.

In Peace's youth the workings of brutalised minds were quite untempered by even the most rudimentary of educations, or contact with other and gentler ways of life. Drink was cheap and strong. Public-houses served round the clock and men and women drank themselves to insensibility, even death sometimes, without hindrance. They slumped where they fell and quick hands rustled through their clothing to seek out the paltriest goods, even tore boots from their feet—for boots could be pawned for a few pence.

As he grew to manhood Charlie Peace became a well known figure in a score of such haunts as this in Sheffield. Like most men of his class and age he was tiny by modern standards, only 5 feet 4 inches in height, but he was a terrier of a man, with a sharp knowing face topped by a mass of unruly brown hair. His eyes were the most striking feature of his face, hazel in colour, full of life, watchful and glittering with something that might be humour, but which had a look, too, that warned people that here was a dangerous being. He would often be greeted with shouts of welcome as he entered with his light, springy step, violin in hand. He would play jigs for dancing, or accompaniments to bellowed songs full of crime and bloodshed and primitive emotions.

Early in his life he drank hard and his taste for women of the lowest sort was insatiable. Later he was to break free of his addiction to drink, in an age when drinking to stupefaction, or insanity, were taken for granted, but he never overcame his reckless desires for women.

Few people born into, or accepted into, those criminal fraternities ever escaped from them. Peace had the sense to reject altogether the false sense of security the outlaw feels in the company of his own kind and to know that the lone wolf ranges farther and wider for longer than his less bold brother in the pack.

He was not yet committed to a life of full-time crime. He was still employed, at least intermittently, by Quaker Smith until 1851, when, at 19, he went to prison for the first time. He and a man of 27, George Campbell, broke into a house in Sheffield and stole two pistols, some diamond rings and other goods. It is an interesting reflection on the lawlessness of the times that a respectable household—the house was occupied by the mother of the Mayor of Sheffield—should contain pistols.

One pistol was sold to a man called Ward, who was a lodger in his mother's house, and the other was pawned in Walker Street, Sheffield. The police have always kept a close eye on pawn shops as a ready way of disposing of stolen property and there seems little doubt that they were "tipped off" by the pawnbroker about this transaction. Peace sold the pawn ticket to another man, who asked Peace to go and redeem the pistol. He did so and was traced by detectives and arrested. Campbell was also arrested and both men were tried for housebreaking. This charge could not be proved and Campbell escaped scot free. Peace was found guilty of receiving the pistol, knowing it to be stolen, and was sent to prison for a month.

The affair is mysterious. The disposal of the goods was clumsily handled. The sentence was very light for a time when offenders, even small children, received long prison terms for petty offences. Perhaps Peace was able to persuade the court that he had been led astray by an older man; perhaps it was felt unfair to deal harshly with him when an older confederate had escaped.

The month was spent at the Wakefield House of Correction. It is likely that during his stay there Peace learned a good deal of the ways of crime and made many useful contacts.

For the next three years Peace seems to have vacillated between crime, working in the rolling mills, and playing his violin for pennies in the Sheffield pubs. He may still have hoped to make his fortune by legitimate means. He joined a society of amateurs who formed themselves into a concert party. Peace played his violin, sang and recited, billing himself as the "Modern Paganini". These keen young men dreamt of success in the professional theatre. They rented a disused theatre at Worksop and staged their first "pro" venture. It was a terrible fiasco. On the second night a party of rowdies pelted them with rotten fruit and broke up the show for ever. The company had some difficulty raising their return fares to Sheffield.

Theatricals had taught Peace some useful lessons. He had worked up an act in which he billed himself as "The Great Ethiopian". One evening, walking home after a concert, but without bothering to wash off the make-up he had used on his face on the stage, he met several acquaintances as he passed down the street where he lived with his mother. It was not lost on him that they failed to recognise him beneath his dark mask. He had learned that in disguise he might well go undetected even by familiars.

There can be no doubt that during these three years Peace committed many house robberies. He had become a daring "portico robber", as cat burglars were then known at a time when the easiest way to climb into a large house was up the porticos, or large stone canopies, over the front doors. In his early years Peace seems to have been an inept criminal, as his prison record was to show. He was known to mix with thieves and to be a "bad hat". How then was he able to avoid detection for so long?

At that time the detection of crime was only in its infancy. Peace was eleven before Sheffield even had a police force. Before that the city, like most of the new towns, had to be content with adaptations of the old watchman system. The watchmen, who were usually elderly, dated from a time when most of the population lived in agricultural communities. As a means of law enforcement the system had collapsed by the end of the eighteenth century, but it was 1829 before the first police force was created in London. It was greeted with fury and rioting from defenders of civil liberty, who saw in the new police an instrument designed for political repression. Sir Robert Peel, who created the police, said bitterly: "It is my task to teach the people that liberty does not consist of having your houses robbed by organised gangs of thieves, and in leaving the principal streets of London in the nightly possession of drunken women and vagabonds."

Gradually the provincial towns, one by one, followed suit and created police forces. Even so the local forces co-operated little, if at all, with one another. The building up of a police system covering the country was developed slowly throughout Peace's life. In his youth the Sheffield force consisted of only a handful of men, helped by night watchmen, and as late as 1856 some parts of the city were unprotected.

The policemen bore little resemblance to the highly trained men of today. They were mainly ex-NCOs from the Army and Navy and their pay was pitiful. An inspector got twenty-five shillings a week, a day constable eighteen shillings a week and a watchman fourteen shillings a week. At this time skilled men in the steel industry were earning twenty-seven shillings a week. A single constable might have to patrol singlehanded a large area, "proceeding without a break at a rate of two-and-a-half miles an hour," for nine hours. It was not an opposition likely to deter a determined lawbreaker. The Constables had plenty to do in merely maintaining the peace. Drink was the national pastime and drunken violence was everywhere. Yet somehow in Sheffield, as in other towns, this underpaid body of men struggled on and imposed some sort of law and order. One can only admire them. They were alone and detested, but there were great pioneer policemen to lead them and the men were steady, when they did not fall themselves victims to the current besetting preoccupation with alcohol. One of the pioneers was Mr. J. Jackson, Chief Constable of Sheffield for many years. Figures collected by him present a startling picture of the Victorian era. Sheffield was then a city of only 135,000 people yet in 1860, when he was already imposing some pattern of order, there were 20 public-houses, 40 beer shops and 2 coffee houses known to be the resorts of thieves and prostitutes. There were 111 known brothels and over 230 prostitutes in the city. An experienced detective estimated recently that there are today perhaps 30 "commercial" women in the city—though he added he defied a stranger to find one.

The city was full of vagrants, 186 people were prosecuted for being without visible means of support. There were 177 men and 90 women who were known criminals, with 53 men and 20 women who were known to be receivers of stolen property.

Peace's long period of impunity from arrest ended in 1854. He was living with his sister, now Mrs. Neil, and 19-year-old Emma James. Emma went into a pawnbroker's shop at Westbar and offered a pair of boots for pledge. There was nothing unusual in this. It was common practice for families to pawn apparel to keep them in food until the next pay day, but for some reason she was detained by the shop staff. It may be that the pawnbroker had been warned by the police to be on the lookout for her, as Mr. Henry Hoole's house at Crooke's Moor had been entered shortly before and seven pairs of boots stolen.

It says something for the younger Peace, who had been waiting outside, that he came forward and claimed the boots. In his turn he was detained and handed over to the police. They discovered that he was wearing a pair of Mr. Hoole's boots.

It was a chance the police had been waiting for. They raided the house where Peace's mother lived in Bailey Field and found a large quantity of stolen goods, including jewellery, the loot of four burglaries. All the houses had been entered by the same method, through an upper bedroom window.

Peace, his sister and James were charged with the crimes and were committed for trial. It was a routine and squalid affair, marred by the fact that Mrs. Neil turned on her brother and admitted that she had pawned some of the goods stolen from the houses, but had done so because Charlie had led her "into a snare". He had said the goods were his own. Peace in his turn said that the goods had been given by his sister to Emma James "whom he was about to marry, in payment of a debt".

They appeared for trial at Doncaster Sessions. They were an unpleasant trio, the women bedraggled, with long dirty hair, and Peace, an undersized furtive creature, in rough workman's clothes, with a muffler about his neck.

The women declined to make a defence but Peace launched into a long rigmarole, gesticulating and whining. He said that Bethley, his old music master, had lived with his sister and given her three children, but had now left her without money. He said that Bethley had sent the goods involved in the charges to her as a payment. He himself had had no idea that they were stolen.

No one was impressed. Peace was sent to prison for four years, the two women for six months. They shuffled down the steps out of the dock and out of Peace's life. Mrs. Neil died four years later at the early age of 33. Emma James was heard of no more; presumably she died in some workhouse or jail in due course; there was not much hope of redemption for the Emma Jameses in the mid-nineteenth century.

Peace now entered the twilight world of prison. To understand something of the man he was to become it is necessary to know the prison system that did so much to create him. He was to spend most of the next fifteen or sixteen years in and out of prison, and was once transported. There can be no doubt that it was prison that turned him eventually into a man prepared to kill rather than face another "lagging".

The organisation of prisons as places of long-term detention came in with the early Victorian era. In the eighteenth century they were not designed to hold men for long terms. Until 1817 the majority of crimes were punishable by death anyway, though in fact comparatively few people were executed. Juries just refused to convict on paltry charges. They might feel a man was guilty, but they did not think he should be hung for what might be merely petty theft. Nonetheless to be charged with a criminal offence was to become the pawn in an awful lottery in which the outcome was death, or freedom. A prisoner might be indicted for a serious crime, encounter a soft-hearted jury and go free. On the other hand a man could run up against a cruel jury, or one that simply did not like his face, and might well die for a trivial misdemeanour. In 1814 a man was hanged for cutting down someone else's cherry tree. In 1831 a boy of nine was executed for arson.

For those reprieved for a variety of reasons, or convicted of the few offences not punishable by death, a jail sentence was often a death sentence anyway. The old prisons were chaos.

The prisoners lived huddled together in communal cells, or dormitories, guarded by turnkeys who had sought the positions with the sole object of making money out of the allowances paid them to keep their charges. Jail fever ran through the buildings, slaughtering prisoners and gaolers alike.

It may be that society, long revulsed by the bloodthirsty sentences of the Law, was finally stung to reform by the fate of the nine-year-old boy hung for arson. In 1832, in the teeth of protests from the Judges that the way was being made open to anarchy, reformers had pushed through legislation substituting prison terms for death sentence in the case of most crimes, except murder.

The population, however, was growing, times were hard, and suddenly the State found itself committed to keep for years a large number of offenders whom shortly before it would have summarily slaughtered. Large numbers were transported to the Colonies overseas, but within twenty years the Colonies were refusing to become dumping grounds for the sweepings of Britain's jails and by 1867 the practice was dying out.

All over Britain the huge prisons, many of which are still in use, began to go up. Into them poured large crowds of desperate men, often for many years at a time, for Her Majesty's Judges, eager like most Victorians to sweep the social dirt beneath the carpet and out of sight, awarded heavy sentences even to first offenders. The authorities running the prisons were forced to inflict harsh regimes out of sheer necessity to maintain order among vast numbers of unruly and ferocious men. The food was atrocious, the discipline severe and enforced by frequent use of the "cat". In 1862 it was agreed that the number of lashes to be awarded to an adult was to be reduced to a maximum of 24, and strokes of the birch for juveniles to a maximum of 12. Flogging could be ordered for offences ranging from mutiny, violence or threats of violence, down to the breaking of windows, "or any other act of gross misconduct or insubordination requiring to be suppressed by extraordinary means". In the same year, too, began efforts to curb the practice of putting men in confinement in the dark and loading them with chains.

The severity of British prisons was notorious, even in Russia. It was sometimes said that for the sentence of death, the prison authorities had substituted a sentence of living death.

Due to the ebb and flow of the influence of various schools of expert opinion some prisons had the "silent" system; under this, prisoners lived and worked together, but were forbidden to speak, or even smile, under pain of heavy penalties. Others confined their charges in single cells; the idea behind this was to give men plenty of opportunity for reflection and hence repentance, and this school gradually assumed the ascendancy.

The beds were hard, blankets were few, the diet was awful, consisting entirely of variations of oatmeal gruel, meat, cocoa, potatoes and bread. There was no fruit, no vegetables, indeed no delicacies of any kind. Men were known to eat candles, and catch worms and frogs to alleviate their hunger.

Work was hard. The lucky men found themselves in the workshops doing useful labour making their own broad arrow uniforms, or uniforms for armed forces. Even picking oakum, or making mailbags was dignified work in comparison with the stone-breaking and useless tasks found to engage the remainder. The treadmill and the crank had a long life before reformers finally had them abolished.

Henry Mayhew, the Quaker reformer, observed of the treadmill: "It remained for the sages of our time to seek to impress men with the sense of the beauty of industry by the invention of an instrument which is specially adapted to render labour inordinately repulsive by making it inordinately useless."

Designed like a giant waterwheel, the treadmill revolved in such a way that the unhappy prisoner on it climbed an endless flight of stairs to nowhere. On the "mill" a man climbed 1,440 steps in every hour and sometimes it was operated so that men did 20 minutes on, 20 minutes off, for six to eight hours a day.

The crank was, if anything, an even more refined instrument for wasting time at the maximum inconvenience to its user. It was an iron box on legs at waist height, with a handle protruding from one end. It turned nothing but a revolution counter and it did not turn easily. In some prisons a man's daily task might be to clock up between ten to twenty thousand revolutions and it would take him all day to do it.

In a pamphlet published by the Humanitarian League, an

ex-prisoner, R.J., wrote of his life in Victorian prisons: "Better to die than go through such misery. I worked myself into a frenzy and I, who had never sworn before, used to curse God and Man."

Being Victorians, those responsible for the prisons felt that they must somehow combine a regime of gruelling hardship to the transgressor's body, with one of moral improvement for his soul. The Chaplain was a powerful man and his reports were all-important. His views on a convict might well weigh heavily in terms of granting or withholding of privileges. The length and severity of periods of solitary confinement, even the granting of remission to be released on ticket-of-leave (introduced about halfway through the century) could be influenced by the chaplain's view of a man. No wonder that more artful convicts strove to be in the chaplain's good books.

Hardened old lags swore that they blessed the day they were sent to prison because it had given them this chance to improve their immortal souls. Chapel services became a competition between men eager to impress upon the chaplain the fervour of their Amens, the enthusiasm of their transports of religious devotion as they rolled their eyes to Heaven for forgiveness.

It was an age, too, of strong religious feeling among the working-classes. Many of the warders were men of sincere Christian faith. They saw nothing incongruous in praying with the charges upon whom they helped to inflict a bodily torment of deprivation and mind-breaking monotony. It was not uncommon for warders, large burly men, to kneel in a cell in prayer with a convict seized by religious emotion—or possibly an ability to simulate it.

The more crafty prisoners learned to distinguish from all others the footsteps of the chaplain approaching their cells and would throw themselves on their knees in order to be "surprised" in an act of devotion.

A number of more shrewd, or less biased observers noted that the combination of harsh regime, in which men had to plot and scheme to obtain even the most ordinary of common comforts or consolations, the seclusion of the single cell with its long lonely hours, and this atmosphere of emotional piety tended to produce a monstrous form of spiritual egotism, an all-absorbing mental selfishness, a form of self hypnosis in which a man tended to assume he had Divine Approval for whatever came into his head.

A number of the more sensitive thinkers of the Victorian era had the convict on their consciences. Indeed he figures as the heroic figure against a cruel society in some of the novels written at that time. In a society which had perhaps a foresight of the fact that in its new sciences and new large cities it was creating a whole way of life with untold implications, the crushed and brutalised convict—the man who had been unable to reconcile himself to the new society—was a warning, a symbol of what increasingly organised communities might do to their nonconformists.

He certainly fared worse than anybody else in Victorian England—with the exception, of course, of those confined in workhouses for the detestable crime of being poor. It was a "Punch" joke that prison discipline should be stiffened by threatening really recalcitrant convicts with the workhouse. Vagrants in these charitable institutions were known to smash windows to effect a transfer to jail.

Like any man above the moron level confined for the first time in the harsh penal barracks, Peace chafed and plotted escape. He was working in the beaming room, manufacturing mats and matting, when one afternoon the door was accidentally left unlocked. He made a dash for it, ran out of the room, and disappeared.

He climbed on to the roof of the prison surgeon's house which was within the confines of the main wall, tore slates from the roof and dropped down into one of the bedrooms. Later a search party found him crouched on top of a wardrobe. He was hauled out and dragged off to solitary confinement. Among the party who found him was a man who was subsequently to win Peace's genuine affection. This was an assistant chaplain, the Rev. J. H. Littlewood.

Later in solitary confinement Peace made a determined effort at suicide. Using a nail he had somehow secreted about himself, he tore a dreadful gash in his throat. He was heard groaning, found semi-conscious by a guard and successfully revived. There seems little doubt that during this period Mr Littlewood was able to bring some comfort to the strange little convict, whose brute nature was so intertwined with sensitive and artistic feelings.

It was Peace's only attempt to escape. There was no remission for good conduct at that time and maybe he felt he had nothing to lose. Whatever the motivations of that attempt to escape, and its dreadful sequel, there can be no doubt the first long term of imprisonment effected a major change in Peace's personality. He seems to have come to regard himself as an enemy of society.

Some years later, Mr. J. Horsfall Turner printed privately *The Annals of Wakefield House of Correction.* In it he makes a tantalising reference to Peace. Referring to certain prisoners he lists Peace and adds that he was "more fitted for an asylum than numbers that are placed therein."

Peace was released in 1858 and resumed his life as a strolling musician. He also had a new source of income, setting himself up as a hawker—a useful blind to the disposal of stolen property, for he immediately began breaking into houses all over the North of England. He seems to have been known in many different towns under a variety of names. This was not so clumsy a device to escape detection as it would be today. Police records were not centralised. Often men captured under one name were able to hide that they had convictions under other names and thus escape with a lighter sentence as a first offender.

Though small, Peace was not ill-favoured as a young man and he seems throughout his life to have exercised a great deal of fascination for many women, often combining business with pleasure. It was his habit to charm young housemaids with his jaunty personality and his whole bag of skills and tricks, his music, his tamed birds and animals—at one time he led about a goat he had trained to perform—his whole air of being a sort of amusing hobgoblin. An incident in Bradford is typical of his method. First attracting her attention with the geegaws in his pedlar's pack, Peace made up to a housemaid employed in a large house just outside the city. So taken was the girl with the genial and entertaining "John Ward", with his merry air, that she snubbed her more worthy young suitor, who was a prosaic shop assistant.

Soon they were "going steady". One night when her employers were away, Mr. Ward suggested that he might call round, bring a bottle of wine and entertain her and the other residents of the servants' hall with a little music and a few recitations.

It was a gay evening. "Mr. Ward" convulsed the company with a series of comic monologues and charmed them with a succession of airs on his violin. He was the life and soul of the party, circulating his wine with a generous hand. He personally was so busy being the jolly centre of the party that he hardly had time to drink himself. He was still as lively as ever when one by one in the small hours of the morning the remainder, including his own "intended" fell into various degrees of drunken slumber. Waking next morning the revellers found that the house had been ransacked of all its valuables and the amusing "Mr. Ward" was seen no more.

Peace spent some time in Bradford. Mr. W. Dunkley, now resident in the Isle of Man, tells how at one time Peace lived in a back-to-back house in Ripon Street, Bradford, which was then owned by Mr. Dunkley's grandfather. During his stay there Peace was well liked in the district, especially by the children who followed him about, for he would play for them on his fiddle or on a tin whistle or a concertina. He was a regular attender at a mission in Otley Road, where, no doubt, his musical abilities were useful in accompanying devotional song.

It is typical of Peace's sly sense of humour that he told Mr. Dunkley's grandfather that his occupation was that of "night watchman".

Peace was now establishing a pattern of behaviour he was to follow all his life—with the exception of one notable period when he was to attempt to put down solid stakes in a community. He would stay a few weeks in a place, "work" a number of the local houses, then move restlessly on to another town. Late in 1858, or early in 1859, he acquired a wife somewhere on his wanderings, even as his father had done before him. A strong part of his nature was his love for his mother and he took for a wife a woman ten years older than himself.

When she met Peace, Hannah Ward was a widow with a six-month-old baby son, Willie. There are two versions of their meeting. One that it was at a Feast in Sheffield, where Peace was providing the music. The other that he met her one day sitting dejectedly on the roadside outside the city with the baby in her arms; that he stopped, struck by the good looks of a woman obviously at the end of her tether and that in response to his gruff "What ails thee, missus", she poured out her sad story to him. Her husband's death had left her destitute with a baby and her sole hope was to walk to Hanley in Staffordshire to find her only living relative. The story goes that touched by her woe Peace took her to a nearby public house, ordered a meal for her and by nightfall she had agreed to throw in her lot with him.

Just where and when they were married it is impossible to say—years later Hannah claimed that Peace had torn up the marriage lines. Whatever the actual legal situation Peace remained socially faithful to his Hannah for the rest of his life and she remained steadfast to him, despite his infidelities with other women. No doubt life with Charlie was hard. Hannah developed into a gaunt, dour woman, but she was astute and capable in preserving her own interests. It is said that she did not know when she became Mrs. Peace that her Charlie was other than a reckless, hard-living hawker and musician. If she did not, she soon learned.

She was already pregnant with the first child of her second marriage when her husband was in the hands of the Law. With the loyalty of her class to her man, she sold up the home they had got together in Sheffield—a tremendous sacrifice to a woman with a child, and a baby due, at a time when homeless women and children could starve in the gutter—to finance his defence.

Peace and another man, Alfred Newton, the owner of a beershop in Spring Street, Sheffield, had been in Manchester on a burgling expedition. Newton was a man of substance—at any rate, he had money in the bank—but perhaps the police were not as strict then as they are now about the granting of licences to run public houses.

The two men got into a house at Rushholme early in June and brought away a large quantity of goods. These they hid for later collection in a sewer in a field near Brightons Grove. When they went back for the swag in August the police were lying in wait. Either they had been tipped off by informers, or had discovered the cache by accident and set a watch. There was a tremendous fight as they tried to arrest the two men and one constable was seriously hurt before the struggling captives could be dragged back to the police station. When they were charged Peace gave his name as George Parker and his occupation as "professor of music".

At Manchester Assizes Peace and Newton put forward an alibi. Peace's mother—described as an "aged woman" though she was in reality only middle-aged—gave evidence that her son had been at home with her every evening during the week of the robbery. Newton claimed that he had been dispensing beer to his customers. The jury were not impressed and Peace was sent to prison for six years and Newton, no doubt as a first offender, for fifteen months.

Peace shuffled down the dock stairs to the gloom of prison and Mrs. Peace had to shift for herself as best she could. Two months later she had their daughter, Jane Ann. She opened a small bow-fronted shop in Kenyon Alley, Sheffield, and contrived to bring up her family with her "wage earner" working for Her Majesty's Government.

Peace served out his time at a number of prisons, at Millbank in London, at Portland, where the hard work of the quarries was dreaded by the convicts, and at Chatham. At Chatham he was mixed up in a mutiny—most likely over food, which was notoriously bad there even for prison fare—and was flogged. As a result he was transferred to the convict settlement at Gibraltar where, with his mates, he worked on building the fortifications.

There is a legend that while at Gibraltar another prisoner incurred Peace's enmity by informing to the authorities and that later this prisoner was found dead at the bottom of a cliff, in circumstances that suggested Peace had thrown him over. Prison records for this time are no longer available, but the story is unlikely. Towards the end of his life Peace made a full confession to his friend, the Rev. Littlewood, at a time in which he had nothing to lose by frankness, and he did not refer to any such incident.

The weary years dragged by, until in 1864 the day came round when he was no longer required to submit to the weekly clip "to the bone" of his hair. Convicts then were marked off physically from other men by hideous shapeless uniforms patterned with broad arrows and with their heads completely shaved. Three weeks before release they were permitted to grow hair again. This time, though he was only 32, Peace's stubble was iron-grey when he heard the prison gate clang behind him in the early morning. During this sentence he had obtained nearly a year's remission for good conduct—a recently introduced system—but he was on ticket-of-leave. While on "ticket" a released convict had, for a fixed time, to report regularly to the police. The idea was to maintain some sort of supervision over known criminals, but it does not seem to have been of much use. The convicts obtained nominal jobs, reported to the police and, in many cases, pursued their criminal activities until recaptured.

Peace went back to live with Hannah in Kenyon Alley and it seems that for a time at least he made a real attempt to live honestly. He operated a small picture-framing business. He certainly worked hard and the enterprise prospered. In 1865 he had two men working for him, with a boy to run errands, and he seemed set fair to become a successful small shopowner, always a way of life that appealed to one side of his nature. The Fates, however, had other things in store for him.

He decided to take a shop in West Street, a much better quarter of the city. It was to prove a mistake and, anyway, his luck seemed to have run out. He became ill with a severe attack of rheumatic fever. He eventually recovered, but from this time on he began to display a new characteristic. He had always been a pugnacious man, well able to hold his own in brawls, but now he developed a tendency to fly into almost maniacal explosions of rage when thwarted. Financial disaster added to his worries.

During his illness the two men he had employed resented taking orders from Mrs. Peace and left. The hawkers, with whom he had carried a good deal of business in Kenyon Alley, were resentful of his move to a better district and began to drift away. The takings in the shop fell, and went on falling. He was on the fringe of bankruptcy and went out of business. These were among the darkest years of his life. He decided to return to his old life and in December 1866, the *Manchester Guardian* reported:—

"George Parker, alias Alexander Mann was indicted for

burglary at Manchester. The Prosecutor, Mr. W. R. Gemmell, lives in Victoria Park, Manchester. On the 29th of August he was disturbed about 4 a.m. by a noise and on his servants going downstairs they found the house had been entered through the kitchen window, that the dining room had been broken open, and that a large number of things and money had been stolen. The prisoner was apprehended a few moments after . . ."

"George Parker" was, of course, Peace. He had committed the crime while fuddled with drink—he had just had nine double whiskies—and was semi-stupefied when seized by Mr. Gemmell's servants. "Working" while drunk was a mistake he never made again. Indeed from that time on he rarely took more than one drink at a time.

The *Guardian* added that "the prisoner made a strong appeal for mercy", but was sentenced to seven years' penal servitude. In fact, Peace made a long grovelling speech, pleading with the Judge to have mercy, not so much for himself, as for his family. It was a whining plea of the type criminals used to make in the faint hope that they might touch some chord in the Judge's heart and perhaps get a year or so knocked off the sentence.

It was a forlorn hope. Though the cases were not proceeded with, there was evidence that he had robbed other houses that same night. The Judge observed wryly, "If the prisoner had been really penitent it was not likely he would have committed the present offence and that in a way that showed he was liable to go to all lengths in housebreaking".

Peace went away to prisons that during his years at liberty had become even more harsh (if that were possible) than during his last imprisonment. In 1862 there had been an outbreak of "garrotting" in London and the big towns. The streets were dark after nightfall and gangs of ruffians waylaid, half-strangled, and robbed scores of people walking back to their suburban homes. The method was for one powerful man to seize the victim round the throat from behind and hold him tight while a confederate rifled his pockets. There was a tremendous uproar—most of the victims were rich and influential—and it led, among other steps, to the creation of a House of Lords committee to inquire into the state of British prisons.

The noble Lords decided that the prisons were not sufficiently penal in character, must be made stricter and become institutions devoted to "hard labour, hard fare and a hard bed". Peace, then, served his sentence under conditions liable to embitter the best of men. He was at Pentonville, Woking and Dartmoor Prisons. What mitigation of the system was obtainable he seems to have obtained. He worked mainly as a tailor and he suggested certain innovations to the sewing machinery that were subsequently adopted in all the convict establishments. He also worked as a carpenter.

Shortly before his release, his only son, christened John Charles Peace, died in infancy. The bereaved father wrote:—

"Farewell, my dear son, by us all beloved.
Thou are gone to dwell in the mansions above,
In the bosom of Jesus who sits on the Throne,
Thou are anxiously awaiting to welcome us home."

The man who could pen this simple piece of piety was now a man in full maturity of his powers. He had become the criminal personality, fully adept at all the miracles of cunning and improvisation such men use in their battle with repressive authority. It is typical that by some method of his own, Peace was able to communicate exactly what he wanted to his wife, through the medium of apparently innocuous official letters. Just how he did this is a secret now lost.

The resourceful Mrs. Peace had once again, when deprived of her husband, opened a shop, at Long Millgate, Manchester, but later, she returned to Sheffield. In 1872 she was living in Orchard Street, Sheffield, in the same street as Peace's mother. Her income was meagre, for she did odd jobs as a charwoman and in the bottling department of a local wine merchant.

On August 9th 1872 householders in Orchard Street, enjoying the warm summer evening outdoors, saw an elderly man walk down the street and knock on the door of old Mrs. Peace's home. A little girl looked out from a nearby house and called out: "Is that you, Father? You mustn't knock there. Grandmother has gone to bed, but come here and see Mother." It was little Jane Peace, now 13. Inside the house Peace found his wife and Willie waiting to greet him.

He had served his last prison sentence. To date his criminal career had been lacking in distinction. He had spent the best years of his manhood in prison for a mere pittance. Now, however, he was truly in his prime and over the next seven years he was to show himself to be one of the most successful criminals in history. He was to maintain a double life, living openly as a small trader and shopkeeper, while during the nights robbing hundreds, if not thousands of homes. He came and went as he pleased despite the fact that he was crippled and marked by easily identifiable wounds, for in addition to his leg injury, he lacked a finger on his left hand.

It cannot be established just when and how Peace lost his finger. Some stories have it that it happened in childhood, others when he was a young man. The greatest likelihood is that it occurred sometime shortly after his release from prison in 1872. It was at this time that he took to carrying firearms—he seems to have been quite determined never to return to prison—and there is strong evidence that the finger was blown off by a firearms accident. Pistols were cruder affairs then and it is quite feasible that he mishandled one and it fired, shooting off the finger.

Part of the secret of his success later in life seems to spring from the fact that he had learned through bitter experience that criminal associates are dangerous friends. The risk of informing is always present. He now began to work on his own, seeking no assistance and ensuring that his methods of disposing of stolen property were only through a trusted handful of people.

From 1872 until 1875 Peace lived and worked, ostensibly as a joiner and picture frame maker from addresses in the Brocco and Scotland Street, Sheffield, though in pursuit of his burglar's targets he ranged over the whole North of England.

Physically he had aged in appearance a great deal during his last prison sentence. He was nearly white-haired and he grew a full set of whiskers to enhance his patriarchal looks. Peace's rapid ageing is interesting. His mother was described as aged when still in her forties. It may be that it was a tendency inherited from her. Moralists have tried to claim that Peace aged because of his life; certainly he was typical of one whose face bears the marks of a depraved and evil life. It is possible that subconsciously Peace found the strain of having to be constantly watchful almost beyond human strength, though his ready coolness in danger and sense of mischief does not suggest an unbearable tension. However it came about he exploited his aged looks to the full, passing himself off whenever politic as an old feeble man. It came in handy in begging lifts on carts when he was travelling about.

It was his habit to slouch as much as possible, bending his back and throwing his head forward to give himself a shrunken stature, but stripped he was well muscled and sinewy, his flesh firm and his frame well knit. His strength was said to be enormous for his size.

He was certainly a tough nut in a rough-and-tumble. His manner was insinuating and he could wheedle persuasively, but at the slightest offence he became an implacable and spiteful foe. On one occasion he mounted a picture for a neighbour and tried to cheat on the price. The man screwed up his courage and remonstrated. The response was a look from Peace of such venomous hatred that he fled. A few mornings later this man was walking, with two other men, down the street when they encountered Peace coming the other way. Peace tried to strike the man and it was only with difficulty that the three men drove him off. At a distance Peace picked up a brick and threw it with such force and accuracy that the man was severely hurt.

Peace used to boast: "I am a match for any three if I know they are coming." Once a drunken workman tried to molest the wizened little elderly gentleman he met on a lonely path. He was startled to find himself seized and flung headlong over a nearby hedge. Another of Peace's boasts was that for a bet he had carried "a twenty-score pig over half a mile".

He also claimed at different times that he rescued a child from a burning house at Armley in Leeds and had saved, at the risk of his own life, a man drowning in a river. Such stories are all part of the legend. It is impossible now to prove, or disprove them. They could be true. He was exceptionally agile and it would be in keeping with his criminal nature to rescue the children—for professional criminals are often fond of children.

The stories of his strength may be exaggerated. Much of his reputation as a fighter may have come from his ferocity, the feeling opponents had that here was a man who would stick at nothing. Robinson, the Constable at Blackheath, was able to handle him, despite a badly injured arm, though Peace was then at an age when strong men often retain their power undiminished. His readiness, too, with firearms later in life does not suggest a man sure of his own physical capacity.

As a burglar he worked with great speed. He never robbed a house "cold", but would visit the scene, days or even weeks earlier, examine the possible means of entrance and, most important, the facilities for a quick getaway. He would also explore the surrounding streets or countryside for the best routes to follow to shake off possible pursuit. Whenever he could he would contrive to get into the house on some legitimate errand first, either as a hawker at the door, as a repairer of clocks and watches, a skill he had acquired from Bethley, his old violin teacher. For such visits he would dress in the appropriate costume, but when actually "working" he discarded the rough clothes and choker of his boyhood and wore respectable "gentleman's" clothing. A favourite disguise for loafing round a district was that of an elderly sea-faring man. He was always careful never to let anyone see his injured hand and wore gloves, the empty finger padded to look as though it held the usual member.

Even without his props of wigs and make-up he had a way of disguising his appearance in a moment. He said himself: "I could dodge any bobby living. I have dodged them many a time. I have walked past them, looked them straight in the face and they have thought I was a mulatto." He had lost a good many of his teeth in prison and because of this was able to thrust out his lower jaw to an amazing extent, at the same part contracting the upper part of his face and forcing a rush of blood up into his face to give him a dark, mottled aspect.

Sometimes he would perform this trick for trusted friends and many years later he performed it for Sir William Edwin Clegg, the famous Sheffield lawyer. Sir William commented: "He certainly could transform his features and make them utterly unrecognizable. He could do this instantaneously. I remember once I expressed surprise that he should go to Scotland Yard (referring to Peace's life at Peckham when he did visit the police headquarters) and he told me he ran no risk and demonstrated how he could change his features. The demonstration was remarkable."

He cunningly employed this device whenever he was photographed, for he feared that one day he might be traced through a likeness. He knew that this trick made him look twelve years older and hideously ugly.

En route to a robbery Peace would carry his burgling kit in a violin case or respectable travelling bag. Often he would arrive in a district, leave the case at the nearest railway station left-luggage office, while he had a last prowl round to ensure the circumstances were favourable for a breaking, collecting the bag again just before he actually went on "the job".

Before starting operations he would pull a pair of socks over the women's boots he always wore at "work". The socks deadened sound and prevented any distinguishing footmarks being made. This, combined with the fact that he had tiny feet, several times persuaded the police that the breaking had been done by a child or a woman. He would stow about his pockets various tools he needed and leave his bag hidden nearby. He said later; "I usually carried an augur, a sharp knife, a jemmy and some screws, and, of course, my revolver."

He would walk quietly up to the house—he moved as silently and quickly as a cat in the darkness—and, if possible, force the hasp of a downstairs window and climb in. If there was no suitable window downstairs, or a handy upstairs window was already open, he would climb hand over hand up the nearest drainpipe to reach it. Window bars were then a common feature of large houses, but Peace could squeeze himself through these, even if the bars were only six or seven inches apart.

Sometimes when he got into a room he would find the door out of it to the rest of the house, was locked. He would use his augur to bore four holes a few inches apart in one of the panels, split the panel to make a hole large enough to put his hand through and unfasten the door. He would then walk quickly through the house, collecting up anything valuable he could see.

Even in strange houses in the dark he could move as silently as a shadow, picking his way up staircases, carefully testing where to stand to prevent creaking. Rifling a room full of sleeping occupants was done so swiftly and carefully that they did not stir. He would take everything of possible value into one room, with a handy window for a speedy exit if necessary, and carefully sort out the objects that were worth taking away. Silver and gold plate he would crush and flatten until he could hide it under his clothing without leaving a suspicious bulge.

During this sorting out he would screw up the door, so that if the alarm was given he would still have time to pick up his loot and get out of the window before the householders could get into the room. He was always careful to be as neat as he could; householders had very little clearing up to do after Peace had called, unlike some burglars who tear everything apart in a frantic effort to scramble together any valuables.

He was so neat that on occasions when a slight noise aroused a sleeping occupant, a quick look into the room revealed nothing amiss, despite the fact that Peace might well be standing concealed, carefully controlling his breathing to make the minimum of noise. A favourite place to hide during such alarms was under tables covered with drapes, or behind curtains. Once he curled himself around the leg of a single-leg table in such a way that he could not be seen below an overhanging tablecloth, and the sleepy householder stumbled back to bed.

With the loot carefully stowed about his pockets, which included an extra large one specially sewn in his coat, Peace would climb out of the house and steal away into the darkness.

The stealth, deftness and quickness of the man is all the more astonishing when one considers that he would ransack not one house like this in a night, but on occasions half-a-dozen, one after the other.

Mention must be made of another skill. Whenever he was out of prison Peace always kept pets, and had considerable ability in animal-training. This was of great use to him professionally for he often encountered watchdogs. While weighing up the chances of burgling a house that was guarded by a dog, he would often succeed in getting to know the dog well enough for it to take food from him. On the night of the robbery he would contrive to give the animal some doped food so that it would sleep soundly.

He continued to exploit his charms for women, though he could not rely on this so readily as in his youth. A number of women, not all of them the sort he met in the rougher quarters of the big cities, were captivated by him. Women, it is said, cannot resist vitality and certainly Peace had all the vitality of evil. He is reported to have told one young woman: "My father was a tamer of wild animals and I have some skill in that line myself and I think, by and by, I will tame you a little."

Despite his absences from his homes in the Brocco and Scotland Street, he remained a devoted family man. Not only did Mr. and Mrs. Peace attend church regularly, but Willie and young Jane were sent to Sunday school. Somehow he struck up an acquaintance with a Rev. Dr. Potter about this time and he is said to have told the clergyman one day: "I believe in God. I believe in the Devil. I fear neither, but I wish my children to love and fear God."

His fondness for children was very real. He would entertain local children with his music and by exhibiting his pets, including his singing bullfinch. In those days school curricula were rather more free and easy than they are now, and on a number of occasions Peace called at schools and offered to entertain the children to a concert of music and recitations. In 1873 he entertained the boys of Highgate School with the Gravediggers' scene from Hamlet, for which their headmaster gave them an afternoon off from their usual studies. His good nature towards children was to stand him in good stead at least once.

One winter afternoon a young schoolmaster in a small town in Yorkshire received a visit from a small, rubber-faced man, carrying a violin case, who offered to give the children a "musical entertainment". The schoolmaster agreed and the little man proceeded to sing, play the violin and recite for hour after hour, until eventually darkness fell outside. Whereupon he somewhat abruptly terminated his show, waved the children goodbye and walked away into the darkness. It was, of course, Peace, who knowing the local police were particularly alert after a robbery in the early hours, had been dodging about the district all morning and had sought this safe refuge until nightfall.

For older friends and acquaintances he had other amusements to offer. He had one room of his home in Scotland Street decked up as a picture gallery, for he had a genuine appreciation of art. Men honoured by an invitation to see the pictures were also shown some pictures of quite startling depravity which their host kept in the room.

It was a pleasant period in the old convict's life. He was moderately prosperous, thanks to the "work" he loved (and it is clear burglary had a fascination for Peace over and above its monetary awards), he had a home and many friends in the city. Indeed he would be greeted with shouts of welcome whenever he cared to drop into one of his favourite taverns. He usually carried with him a curious piece of ingenuity he had invented and made himself—a walking stick he could convert into a one-string fiddle—and if he was in the mood he would oblige with a tune or two.

Unhappily for a man of still ardent desires Mrs. Peace was getting on, but there were plenty more fish in the sea, surely for a man who knew how to make a woman's heart flutter.

CHAPTER THREE

In 1875 Peace and his family moved into a small terraced house 40, Victoria Place, Britannia Road, Darnall. It was to be the most fateful of Peace's many changes of address. Next door but one, at No. 36, were living a Mr. and Mrs. Arthur Dyson, lately returned from America with their small son, then aged five.

Darnall is now part of modern industrial Sheffield, but in those days it was more of a village some miles east of the city surrounded by pleasant countryside. There is no doubt that something about it held a special appeal for the battered ex-convict. Darnall was always to hold a treasured place in his heart, though even in his own time the city was to engulf it. He would have liked to have gone on living there indefinitely, yet his own nature and its compulsions were to drive him from this haven within a few short months, for a few weeks after his arrival at the modest little house he was hopelessly infatuated with Mrs. Dyson.

Using his customary front as a combination of pedlar, picture framer and wood carver, Peace travelled from Darnall over a wide area of Yorkshire and the North, robbing a whole series of houses with impunity. To most of his new neighbours he appeared an amiable elderly man, not overly prosperous, but a pleasant enough fellow in a rough West Riding sort of way. His home was modestly, even humbly furnished, though he was a great deal more prosperous—thanks to his large number of successful "jobs"—than the family's way of life suggested, for Mrs. Peace was still washing bottles at the wine merchants and Willie ran errands for a grocer.

Very early in his new life at Darnall Peace did have one unpleasant shock. Walking through the village one day he was horrified to find himself face to face with the Rev. Littlewood, one-time Chaplain at Wakefield House of Correction, now Vicar of Darnall. He was off his guard and could only make a quick, unsuccessful attempt to avert his face to avoid recognition. The Vicar, however, gave him a cheerful salute before going on his way. Exposure and the break-up of this contented pattern of life must surely follow.

In fact, the Rev. Littlewood had not made any particular mental note of him. Littlewood, a sturdy Derbyshire farmer's son, an ex-amateur wrestler and a frank forthright man, had a ready capacity for getting on friendly terms with the cottagers in his Parish. This was not so common an attribute among Anglican clergymen of that time. Mostly highly educated products of expensive homes, they were apt to be ill at ease with their rough charges. The Rev. Littlewood, however, coming as he did from the fresh air and beauty of the Derbyshire countryside, had early been appalled by the conditions among "the grinders"—the nickname for workers in the steel trades—and had dedicated himself to work among them. He was ardent, he was a man of wide sympathies and had set himself to win the friendship of these rough and ready people. Seeing a man looking at him with something like recognition he had greeted him. He did not identify Peace as the former lag from Wakefield.

Peace hurried home in a ferment of worry. Something must be done. He changed into his Sunday-best suit, put on the beloved hard collar of the time and hurried to the Vicarage. Meekly, hat in hand, he craved an audience with the Vicar. A brief wait in the hall and he was ushered into the study. In a torrent of words he pleaded with the Vicar to preserve his secret, repeating over and over again that he had reformed and begging the clergyman to have mercy on his family.

Gravely the Rev. Littlewood listened. "Very well, Peace," he said, "I will say nothing to anybody provided you show me your reformation is genuine. I shall expect you and your family to attend Divine Worship regularly and live soberly and properly."

A flood of protestation followed and the bargain was struck. Peace left the Vicarage with a jaunty air of self-satisfaction. It was a bargain he was only too happy to keep—at least on the surface. More than that he genuinely liked the warm-hearted clergyman.

Every Sunday Peace and his family were lodged in pews in

the church where the Vicar could not fail to see them, Peace presenting a picture of sturdy rectitude. No voice spoke the Amens with more feeling than the "reformed burglar", though on many a Sunday morning he must have been struggling to combat tiredness due to a hectic night at work. Mrs. Peace and little Jane joined the Bible classes run by Mrs. Littlewood for the cottage parishioners. Mrs. Littlewood was somewhat surprised that Mrs. Peace and her daughter appeared so often in expensive clothes, including rich-looking furs, furs in those days being very much the prerogative of the wealthy.

Mrs. Peace and Jane seemed so grateful for Mrs. Littlewood's help and guidance that they were soon deep in the activities among women in the district. In token of their esteem they presented the Vicar's wife with a most ingenious little toy to help amuse the Sunday school children. It was a mechanical bird which, mounted on a stick, could be wound up and it would then sing a few notes.

Charlie set himself out to be at his most winning with the Vicar. He was genuinely interested in theology and he spent many happy hours closeted with the Vicar in his study. The Rev. Littlewood often said later that few laymen knew their Bible as well as Peace. It was not long before Peace had been recruited to help out teaching at the Sunday school, which he did with great success.

It was a testimonial to Peace's charm, when he cared to exert it, that he so completely persuaded the Vicar of his sincere desire to make a new life. The Rev. Littlewood was nobody's fool and his service in the prisons had acquainted him with the plausibility of old lags. "Peace was one of the most interesting men I have ever met and I shall always believe he had much good in him," he told friends in later years.

He did have one shock, however, when one morning the Sunday school clock was missing. He immediately sought out Peace. "Peace," he demanded, "what have you done with my clock?"

The new Sunday school teacher burst into a stream of denials of any guilt in the removal of the timepiece. The Vicar was not altogether satisfied, but assuming that it was the work of a fit of absent-mindedness, a mere mechanical twitch of well rehearsed light fingers, he decided to say no more. He was anyway too honest a man to find Peace guilty without proper proof. But after this there was a certain coolness in his relations with Peace.

A long time afterwards when the time came for Peace to make a full confession of his many misdeeds to the Vicar he referred to the incident. It says much for his regard for Littlewood that he should remember such an incident in a lifetime of crime only shortly before he was due to be executed.

"I understand," he told the Vicar, "that you still have the impression that I stole the clock from your day-schools."

"I have that impression," the Vicar replied.

"I thought you had and this has caused me much grief and pain for I can assure you I have so much respect for you personally that I would rather have given you a clock, and much more besides than have stolen it. At the time your clock was stolen I had reason to believe that it was taken by some colliers I knew."

The Vicar thought for a moment. Finally he said: "Peace, I am convinced that you did not take the clock. I cannot believe that you dare deny it now in your position, if you really did."

Peace burst into tears of relief.

The sincerity of his protestation of willingness to give to the Vicar, rather than take from him, is substantiated by the fact that after Peace's Darnall idyll had been broken up and he was once again a hunted man, the Vicar discovered that the Peace family had indeed been generous in presenting his wife with the mechanical singing bird. It turned out to be a rare work of art—one of only two in the country—and very valuable for under its disguising coat of paint it was made of pure gold. Always a connoisseur of rare *objets d'art*, Charlie had "won" it one night from a house in Manchester, to which, of course, the Vicar returned it.

Despite the slight coolness with the Vicar over the clock Peace's life in Darnall was still flowing on a pleasant course. He had his "work", his theological duties among the young, his garden, in which he took a keen interest, and, most important, he was now head-over-heels in love with his neighbour, Mrs. Dyson.

Mrs. Catherine Dyson was what Victorians called "a fine

looking woman". While not exactly pretty, she was tall, well built, with fine rosy cheeks and raven black hair, which she wore fashionably braided and neatly coiled upon her head. She was 25 years old when Peace met her and spoke with a fascinating Irish brogue, with a faint undertone of American drawl. She was, as she was to prove, a woman of spirit.

She was born in Ireland, but when she was 15 had gone to live with a married sister in Cleveland, Ohio. In Cleveland she had met Arthur Dyson, from Sheffield. He was a railway engineer and was in America on the staff of the Atlantic and Great Western Railway.

Though some years older than the mettlesome Irish girl Dyson had been ardent and they were married shortly afterwards. Dyson was an immensely large man, nearly six-and-a-half feet tall, and in his youth of adventurous disposition. After the marriage the couple travelled about America helping to build the railway system that was to open up the continent.

This was how Mrs. Dyson subsequently described* their life together. "He (Dyson) became the engineer of lines in process of construction and his last engagement in America was as superintendent engineer of the magnificent bridge which spans the Mississippi, and here his health broke down. He had often been compelled to lead a very rough life and it began to tell. His duties made that necessary, for the railways on which he was engaged opened up quite new country. The life, however, had many charms for me. I am a good hand at driving and am fond of horses.

"I always used to drive Mr. Dyson. He used often to say that I could drive better than he, and he would sit back in the buggy while I held the reins and sent the horses along. I liked the excitement of driving him to and from his work and especially when we were in new country and he was out surveying. I have driven him through forests where there were bears and over creeks swollen by floods. The horses often had to swim.

"I remember on one occasion sending the horses and the buggy over a river and then coming over myself on a piece of timber . . .

"Afraid. Not I. I did not know then what fear was. Besides I have a good deal of courage—I think I have gone through

* in an interview with the *Sheffield Independent*.

sufficient of late to show that . . . To be in positions attendant with danger caused me not fear, but a kind of excitement, which if not always pleasurable, certainly possessed some kind of fascination."

It was after Mr. Dyson's health had broken down that the couple returned to Dyson's native Sheffield with their son. Mr. Dyson obtained employment with the railway—a special desk having to be built for him because of his great size. He was now 48 years old, had been married for nine years and there is evidence that the marriage was suffering a bad patch. On one occasion after their return to Sheffield the police had had to be called in after a dispute in which Mrs. Dyson had hit her husband with a poker—and he had hit back.

Dyson is the most tragic figure in the Peace story and yet he remains a shadowy one. He was a man of genteel tastes and some pretensions to refinement. As he approached 50 he undoubtedly preferred a quiet life and his health was not good. This may have sat a little heavily upon the much younger wife, who had so enjoyed her exciting life in America.

Dyson was described by contemporaries both as athletic and robust, and as delicate despite his giant frame. It is likely that he had been a man of hardy and enterprising character, but due to ill health and disappointment in his chosen career had lost something of his original vitality. Life had worn him down. He was on occasions to accept the grossest insults from Peace, yet he was to show himself a man of great courage.

It seems likely that Peace was enamoured of Mrs. Dyson from the first, and she, with her liking for the dangerous, found him an exciting suitor. He set about courting her in an oblique and cunning fashion, working on the principle that if you want to have an affair with the wife, first make a friend of the husband. Peace set out to win over Mr. Dyson. He also worked out a flanking attack on her woman's heart by showing great interest in her small son. Every morning as Mr. Dyson set out for his office, and when he returned at night, he "accidentally" ran into his new neighbour, Mr. Peace, who would greet him with hearty "Good mornings" or "Good evenings" and friendly references to the weather. In common civility Dyson would return the greetings.

The small Dyson boy naturally played in the street before

the houses and his eye was taken by Mr. Peace's well trained parrots and pigeons set out in their cages upon the wall in front of the house. He hung back shyly, but the kindly white-whiskered owner of the fascinating birds suggested that he step forward for a closer look.

That evening as Mr. Dyson came home Peace knocked politely at his door and asked if he might take the boy inside his own home to see his other pets. The Dysons agreed. Conversation began and a tentative friendship struck up. It was not long before Peace was a regular visitor of the Dysons.

In an interview with a *Sheffield Independent* reporter, Mrs. Dyson gave a vivid, if somewhat one-sided account, of the family's relationship with the genial pet-fancier. She contrived throughout the interview to give an impression of herself as a model wife and mother, she said: "Our impression was that he was a really nice old man. He was plausibility itself. He appeared to be simply a picture framer in anything but good circumstances. . . ."

Mr. Dyson had soon begun to tire of the friendship. "My husband had travelled and could converse well upon many subjects, but Peace soon began to show himself anything but a gentleman." It appeared that Peace had shown Mr. Dyson some obscene pictures—to the latter's distress—and suggested, with a number of knowing nods and winks that they might make an expedition together to see the sights of the town, the "sights" in this context being the brothels and disorderly houses. Mr. Dyson had refused somewhat indignantly and had issued the family edict that relationship must be broken off with Peace.

"But we couldn't get rid of him. He would drop in when we were sitting down to tea and we were compelled to ask him to have a cup. His constant visits to the house became intolerable to us."

Matters came to a head and Peace was informed, stiffly, that his presence was no longer welcome.

"He became awfully impudent. He would, for instance, stand on the doorstep and listen through the keyhole or look through the window at us. I can hardly describe all that he did to annoy us after he was informed he was not wanted at our house. He would come and stand outside the window at night and look in, leering all the while. He would come across you at all turns and leer in your face in a manner that was frightful."

Mrs. Dyson added that for her part she would have taken the law into her own hands and dealt hardly with Peace—indeed she claimed that on one occasion she had "thrashed" him for insulting her—but Mr. Dyson had ordered her to ignore him.

It seemed that the purport of Peace's behaviour, she told the reporter, was to persuade her to leave her husband and run away with Peace. He had promised her that if she did so he would set her up in a shop in Manchester, spend £50 on fitments and she could build a thriving business in the cigar or picture trade. She was to live like a lady, decked in fine clothes and jewellery. On one occasion it appeared Peace had actually offered her a sealskin jacket and some yards of fine silk, but she had told him, "make a present of them to your wife and daughter".

Furthermore in response to the bait that she might live like a lady she had rounded on him with: "Thank you. I have always lived like one and shall continue to do so quite independently of you."

There can be no doubt that eventually Peace's excitement-tinged fascination for Mrs. Dyson led to her conceiving an authentic terror of him. "He had a way of creeping and crawling about, and coming upon you suddenly unawares. I cannot describe to you how he seemed to wriggle himself inside a door, or the terrible expression of his face. He seemed more like an evil spirit than a man. I used to be especially afraid of him at nights because he had a habit of continually prowling about the house and turning up suddenly. He would, too, assume all sorts of disguises. He used to boast how effectually he could disguise himself. He once said 'I am never beaten when I have made up my mind. If I make up my mind to a thing I am bound to have it, even if it cost me my life'."

A dreadful picture of an innocent couple persecuted by a monster, but as time went by, and more light was thrown on her exact relationship with Peace, Mrs. Dyson was forced to qualify her picture of her own behaviour a great deal. She may have ended by hating Peace as vehemently as she told the reporter, but there was another side to it all. In the end she found herself engaged in a contest in open court with one of the shrewdest barristers of the day in an attempt to preserve her chosen casting as a model wife, blameless in her traffic with other men, especially with the "monster" Peace.

To the end Peace was to maintain that Mrs. Dyson became his mistress and that they had secret meetings in the garret of an empty house between their two homes in Darnall. There can be no doubt that they went out together and that she accompanied him to music halls and public-houses, and on one outing she was seen to be "slightly inebriated".

There were banked fires beneath the calm exterior of the young wife and mother. She was married to an older, and ailing man. Peace, with his immense vitality, was attractive. Indeed a certain kind of woman is especially attracted to the aura of a rogue. Peace was generous and, not working conventional hours, had endless time to indulge in an intrigue.

One can imagine that an affair with Peace—this strange little man who could so excitingly combine a flattering deference with an underlying hint of steel beneath—would appeal to her femininity. The excitement of a conspiracy, the sense of adventure in secret meetings, would thrill Mrs. Dyson's fondness for adventure, given so little outlet in a respectable English environment.

If they did have an affair it could only end in disruption and hatred. Neither were of the temperament to bow out of a passionate sexual escapade quietly and discreetly. In a modern setting an affair between two such natures would have ended in scenes, reconciliations, more scenes, denunciations and concluded in a grand explosion of bitter farewells. The dangerous temper of the matter could be thus dispelled in the open air of a society adjusted to the idea that a man and woman may have a short-lived, if tempestuous relationship. In the stifling air of Victorian morality the wounds could only fester in the dark.

It may well be that Mrs. Dyson was not the first woman to imagine that she could take the tiger of a powerful masculinity by the tail and live to tell of it without wounds; nor was Peace the first middle-aged man who, finding his sexuality as ardent as ever, as age diminished his appeal, entered into a light-hearted affair only to find that a man does not in middle age love 'em and leave 'em with the ready abandon of youth.

Time now was not on his side and he may have feared that he would not find another young woman to warm him against the lengthening shadows of age.

Whether or not Peace was a man forcing unwanted attentions on a woman, who had led him on, at least part of the way, or whether he was a man furious at the shock to his vanity of being finally thrown over in favour of the despised husband, one thing is sure. By July 1876 Dyson and Peace were on thoroughly bad terms.

In a strangely ineffectual action for a man used to dealing with the hardships of pioneering railway building, Dyson scribbled a message "Charles Peace is requested not to interfere with my family" on one of his visiting cards and threw it into Peace's garden. It was like throwing a meatball to placate a ravening tiger. Peace's fury against Dyson mounted to near madness.

He made desperate attempts to persuade Mrs. Dyson to run away with him, but to no avail. Day after day he exhibited his birds upon his wall, forcing them through the little repertoire of tricks he had taught them, in a pathetic bid to signal his love for her. The streak of violence in his nature stirred his brain into a cauldron of fury, against the Dysons, against anybody, against life.

His mother, who normally was the recipient of his kindlier moods, told him that he must give up Mrs. Dyson. "That woman means only trouble." He flung out of the house and stopped visiting her. Mrs. Peace, Willie and Jane knew better than to raise the subject. Once Jane spoke slightingly of Mrs. Dyson. Her father struck her a heavy blow in the face and stormed out of the house.

His behaviour began to take on the aspects of lunacy. He was summoned at this time for non-payment of his water rate. He visited the Rating Office and carried on like a madman, seething with threats against the officials. He began to follow the unhappy Mr. Dyson about in the streets, hurling threats and oaths at him. Dyson maintained a dignified silence, but consulted a solicitor. The solicitor told him there was nothing he could do until Peace did something that brought himself within the stretch of the law.

On July 1st Peace was lurking about in the roadway when

Dyson returned home from work. He screamed the grossest insults at the unfortunate railwayman. Maddened by Dyson's refusal to take any notice of him Peace followed his rival down the street, snatching at his heels in an effort to trip him forward on his face. Mustering what dignity he could Dyson walked on.

It is perhaps of some significance that Peace, combatant in any number of fights in his youth, made no direct attempt to assault the huge engineer. It may be that he feared that Dyson might prove a harder nut to crack than his refusal to take umbrage suggested. Dyson reached his own home and turned in to his front door, still without showing the slightest recognition of Peace's existence.

Peace slunk away, but within a short while was back again lurking in the street. He was in the grip of such an obsession that he was beginning to be utterly neglectful of the caution an ex-convict must observe.

About nine or ten o'clock the same evening Mrs. Dyson was standing outside the house talking with some neighbours, a Mr. and Mrs. Sykes, and her particular feminine friend in the district, Mrs. Padmore. Their conversation faltered and trailed off as Peace shuffled up out of the deepening twilight. Catherine Dyson was not easily frightened. "Why do you annoy my husband in the way you do?"

Peace went into a sort of frenzy. He jerked a revolver from his jacket pocket and pointed it at Mrs. Dyson's head. "I will blow your bloody brains out and your bloody husband's too."

Despite the muzzle only a few inches from her face, Mrs. Dyson did not move. Peace stood irresolute for a moment, his face working with passion, then with an oath he pocketed his weapon and turned to make off. A few paces away, he turned on his heel and walked back to the silent group. He spoke to James Sykes. "Now Jim, you are a witness that she struck me with a life preserver."

Courageously Sykes replied that he had been a witness to Peace's threat to shoot Mrs. Dyson. Peace darted a look of fury at him, but turned away again. "I have got enough ammunition here to do for half-a-dozen of you." He walked away into his own house.

It says much for the hardiness of the nerves of Victorian women that they did not shriek or faint, particularly as Mrs.

Sykes was heavily pregnant and indeed bore a son a few days later.

Peace had given the Dysons the opening they had been waiting for. The next morning Mrs. Dyson attended the local Magistrates' Court and took out a summons against Peace, charging him to appear before the court to give reason why he should not leave her and her husband in peace.

It was a serious matter to a man with Peace's long criminal record. He had shown himself to have been carrying firearms and to have threatened a woman's life. He did not appear in court on the day set aside and a warrant was issued for his arrest. The police called at his home to arrest him, but he had gone. He had created a haven and by his own inability to control his passions had destroyed it.

Shortly afterwards Mrs. Peace and the rest of the family moved away to open an eating-house in Collier Street, Hull. The capital, of course, came from Peace's nocturnal forays. Indeed in the period just before this time Sheffield detectives had been puzzled by the number of raids in which the burglar had made off with large quantities of food from rifled shops and warehouses. This was Peace's unique way of entering the catering trade. He had been stocking up.

The Dysons heaved a sigh of relief. The nerve-racking persecution was now surely finished. They found that it had only just begun.

Three letters arrived from Peace, all postmarked Hamburg in Germany. They were rambling abusive letters to Mrs. Dyson, alternatively pleading with her not to hate him because he loved her and threatening all kinds of vile retaliation if she did not withdraw the summons.

There are two theories about these letters, one that Peace asked a sailor on a Hull-Hamburg steamer to post them for him in Germany; the other that he did visit Germany a number of times. During his lifetime Peace stole literally sackfuls of silverware, jewellery and other valuables. The outstanding mystery of his life—just how he disposed of his loot—has never been solved. He must have dealt regularly with a "fence" or receiver of stolen goods. It was a secret he never revealed. It is doubtful if even Mrs. Peace knew.

The letters the Dysons did their best to ignore, but the persecution was not to end merely with abusive letters. Peace was certainly back in England, even if he was abroad after leaving Darnall, late in July. He had gone to "work some houses" in Manchester.

He took lodgings in the city and on the night of August 1st set out after dark to walk to the exclusive residential district of Whalley Range, then on the fringes of the Manchester urban sprawl. He had marked out a house that he felt certain would yield a good return. It was large, stood in its own grounds and there were a number of routes by which he could reach it in the dark without risk of detection.

It was a dark night when he set out and raining slightly, but as he made his way at a steady pace towards his target the rain stopped. He walked through the streets quite openly. He was dressed with some care and presented an eminently respectable appearance. He once said: "Policemen do not bother you if they note you are dressed like a gentleman." This would seem nonsense today in an age of conformity in dress due to mass manufacturing techniques, but in Victorian years men dressed according to their station. A labourer looked like a labourer, a clerk like a clerk and a gentleman like a man of means.

Peace was quite at ease. He had his pistol in his pocket if anybody dared to interfere with him. He was even prepared to tackle—as he described them—"obstinate Manchester policemen". He passed several on his way to work, bidding them a civil "Good night". Let them stop him if they dared. He was not to be trifled with. . . .

Shortly before midnight young Police Constable Nicholas Cock was walking along Chorlton-cum-Hardy Road towards Whalley Range. Cock was a 20-year-old ex-miner from Durham, who had joined the Force only nine months before. He was smallish for a policeman in those days, being only five feet eight or nine inches tall, but he made up for his lack of inches with zeal. There were indeed those in his district who said that young Cock, or "the little Bobby" as they dubbed him, was too zealous. It may be that being new to the work Cock did sometimes press a matter rather strongly where an older man might have turned a discreetly blind eye. He had, perhaps, the excusable fault of inexperience. He was a brave and active man, but that evening before going on duty he had told some of his mates that he was not happy about the night that lay ahead and that he had a premonition something dreadful was going to happen. Nonetheless he had resolutely insisted on going on his patrol.

When he heard footsteps behind him on the dark road as he made his way along Chorlton-cum-Hardy Road he turned somewhat nervously. That very morning he had appeared in court to give evidence in a case of drunkenness. Three Irish brothers, called Habron, or Hebron, lived and worked at Deakin's Nurseries just off the road he was now travelling. He had had occasion to charge the brothers with disorderly conduct after they had been drinking. The three men had been very angry. One brother had appeared in court that morning, and afterwards had threatened to shoot him.

He had been upset and told his superior, Superintendent Bent, about the threat, but Bent had pooh-poohed any real danger, saying "threatened men live long". He knew the Superintendent was a very experienced man and he should know. He didn't think the Habrons would really do anything. They were good workmen and normally steady enough fellows. Still he did not terribly want to meet them tonight, especially if they had been drinking. Best to give them time to cool down.

He was not, however, a man to shirk danger, so he waited as the footsteps came up to him. In the light of a street lamp he saw it was an acquaintance, another young man, Mr. John Massey Simpson, a law student, who also lived nearby. Simpson gave him a friendly greeting and the two young men walked along together towards the spot where Chorlton-cum-Hardy Road met Upper Chorlton Road and Seymour Grove. There was a triangle of grass at this meeting of the three roads. There was also a small private road leading off this road junction leading down to Firs Farm and from there a man could get to the back of Deakin's Nurseries.

Cock and Simpson stood talking near to the junction, at a place known as the jutting stone at West Point. There was a street lamp at the corner of the private road to Firs Farm and shortly afterwards they saw Police Constable Beanland walk past this from the direction of Chorlton Road. It was now just after midnight. The three men stood talking for five or six minutes.

Simpson was to say later that while they were still talking he saw a man come out of the darkness into the light of the lamp, cross the road, hesitate for a second, then turn up into the darkness of Seymour Grove. He said he had seen the man quite clearly. He was wearing a brown or dark coat and a pot hat. He did not see the face in the shadow of the hat.

Beanland, on the other hand, said he saw nobody while the conversation was going on, but after Simpson had said goodbye and gone off home, he had seen a man come down Upper Chorlton Road, walking quickly. This man, said Beanland, stopped under the lamp, then turned away up Seymour Grove. He did not see the man clearly, but thought him to be young and fresh-complexioned.

"Who's that man?" he asked Cock. Cock didn't know, but said it might be one of the sons of a Mr. Gratrix who lived in the first big house up Seymour Grove. Beanland replied that he didn't like the look of him. He had seemed uneasy at seeing the police.

Beanland bent down to get a better look along Seymour Grove, but there was no sign of the man having gone past the gate to Mr. Gratrix's big detached house. "I'll go and see who he is," he told Cock and walked off quickly down Seymour Grove. Cock stood waiting just outside the garden wall of the house. He heard Beanland turn into Mr. Gratrix's drive.

All his keen young policeman's blood was up at the thought of a possible capture. Two horse-and-carts, night soil wagons using the late night streets to avoid offence to passers-by, rumbled past him.

Out of the darkness came a man . . . "Hey, you!" he called, moving forward . . .

Beanland walked up past Gratrix's gate, which was standing open. He went up the drive shining his bullseye lantern ahead of him. He tested the front door. It was secure. He flashed his light on the windows. All seemed in order. He was just turning to walk back to the road when, from the other side of the garden wall, he saw two quick flashes and the slam-slam of pistol shots. There was a groan, "Oh, murder, murder, I'm shot. I'm shot" . . .

Out in the street Cock stumbled a few paces, blood jetting from a hole in his uniform tunic just near the heart. He fell heavily against the wall and lay, stirring feebly, as Beanland and Simpson, who had heard the shots and hurried back, bent over him. Beanland blew a blast on his police whistle, then began to give what help he could to his injured mate. Police Constable William Ewen, alerted by the whistle, hurried up from further down Seymour Grove. Bending down over Cock he asked: "Who shot you?"

Cock whispered faintly: "I don't know", then lapsed into unconsciousness.

The two horses pulling the carts had bolted on hearing the shots, but their drivers had managed to pull them up and drive back to the scene. Cock was lifted, groaning, into the back of one of the carts and driven to the home of the nearest surgeon, Dr. John Dill. On the way they passed Police Sergeant Moses Thompson. He jumped into the cart and helped to prop up the wounded man. They carried him into the surgeon's house and Dr. Dill hurriedly probed for the bullet, in what he knew was a futile race against time. One look at Cock had shown him that the young constable was mortally hurt.

Within a few minutes Superintendent Bent arrived by cab. He had no doubt what he should do. Only a few hours earlier he had laughed in a fatherly way when Cock had told him of threats to shoot him. Now he was looking down as the harsh gaslight fell on the white face of the young man whose life blood was draining away. He issued a few crisp orders to the policemen gathered outside Dr. Dill's home. He was personally going to "take" the Habrons. The Sinn Fein, fighting for Irish self-government, was active in Britain and Ireland. He would take no chances with armed Irishmen, but he was going to collar those brothers if it was the last thing he ever did.

He used the cab to drive back to the place where Cock had been shot. He left it there and he, and a party of other policemen, big men moving silently in the dark, walked down the private road, round Firs Farm and up to Mr. Deakin's home. They could see the outhouse nearby, where Bent knew the three men he had come to get made their home. He was going to have to go into that dark place after three men he firmly believed had just committed a brutal murder. Well, if it had to be done it would be done. Bent was not a man to send in a subordinate after dangerous men while he hung back. He stood watching the outhouse, planning what to do, quickly but calmly. Did he see a light suddenly show in one of the outhouse windows, a light quickly extinguished?

"Just keep a look out," he told his men and made his way to Mr. Deakin's front door. As quietly as he could he knocked up the nurseryman and told him that Cock had been shot. Deakin was horrified. "I told them to let it drop," he said, "Oh my God, if it is any of these men it is that young one as he has the most abominable temper of any man I ever knew in my life."

"Mr. Deakin, I feel that these men may shoot rather than be taken," Superintendent Bent told him, "I want you to go to their door and ask for it to be opened. Then I will come past you and get in. I must warn you it may be dangerous."

After what the Superintendent later described as "some little hesitation", Mr. Deakin consented to do what he was asked. The two men made their way towards the outhouse, other policemen falling in behind them. Bent and Inspector Whillan stood just behind Deakin as he knocked on the outhouse door. There was no sign of movement within. Deakin knocked again. Silence. Another knock—there was a mumble from within and the door was half opened. Pushing Deakin out of the way, Bent rushed into the hut, Inspector Whillan close behind him. In the harsh light of their lanterns they could see the three brothers huddled together in one large bed. There was no fight in them.

In response to curt orders from Bent they climbed one by one naked from the bed, huddled trembling into their clothes, then, handcuffed, were taken to Old Trafford Police Station and charged with the murder of Cock.

About this time Peace was walking along the railway line about two miles the Manchester side of Old Trafford Police Station. It was an old trick of his for moving about at night. There was nobody to see him making his way along the track and he could always hide by lying down whenever a train passed.

He stepped out quickly in the darkness, moving surefootedly from sleeper to sleeper. When he came to a roadway running beside the line, he stopped and looked quickly around. All was quiet. He stepped jauntily out into the road and began to walk towards his lodgings in Manchester.

The next few weeks were terrible ones for the Habron brothers. They appeared before the Magistrates, were remanded in custody, and two of them were committed for trial. There was no case against one brother, Frank, who was consequently discharged. Things looked very black though for 23-year-old John and "the young one", William, who was only 18. Nobody would listen to their protestations that they knew nothing of the shooting of Police Constable Cock.

Back in Sheffield the Dysons were also becoming steadily more uneasy as the days went by.

Reports were relayed to them that Peace had been seen lurking about the district. Mrs. Padmore said she had seen an old woman acting suspiciously in Britannia Road, hanging about outside the Dysons' home. Thinking the old woman was possibly a thief on the lookout for an opportunity to steal she had contrived to walk past her and take a good look. She was sure she had seen what looked like white whiskers tucked away in the folds of the shawl over the woman's head—a harder look and she had been convinced the "old woman" was none other than Peace.

The Dysons were all the more perturbed because, since their failure to arrest Peace on the warrant, the Police had told them something of the man. They knew now they were dealing not with a lovesick elderly workman, but a dangerous criminal.

Peace was indeed hanging about Darnell, whenever urgent business did not require his attention elsewhere. On those occasions he had told a young miner, William Bolsover, who was the childhood sweetheart of his daughter, to keep an eye on the Dysons for him.

By the October the Dysons, or certainly Mr. Dyson, had had enough. Mr. Dyson did not care for Darnall, which was becoming a somewhat drab working-class area as Sheffield spread its tentacles outward. On the 25th of that month Bolsover, on guard, saw a furniture van outside the Dysons' house.

When it was loaded he set out to follow it to its destination. It went straight through the centre of the city and out the other side on the Ecclesall Road, to the west. He was shuffling along in the rear of the heavily laden vehicle when, to his astonishment, Peace came out of a side road and also took up the pursuit. Peace grinned knowingly, but volunteered no information about his sudden presence.

It was getting dark by the time the van arrived outside a terraced house, one of seven known as Banner Cross Terrace by reason of the Banner Cross Hotel at one end of the block. The Dysons' new home was second in the block at the far end from the hotel, the first being run as a sort of small shop. The removal men started offloading and, in answer to a query by Peace, said that the master and mistress of the house would be along directly as they were coming by rail from Darnall.

Bolsover lounged about in the roadway while Peace went into the shop and spoke to the proprietors, Mr. and Mrs. Gregory. He told Gregory he had some confidential information for him. To Mr. Gregory's amazement he then poured out a diatribe against the Dysons, the new neighbours, saying they were "bad people" and he had letters to prove it. These new neighbours, he said, would get into debt if they could and then not pay, if they could avoid doing so.

Then he walked out of the shop, impudently pushed past the removal men, sauntered into the Dysons' new home and walked through the rooms. He noted that there was a common yard behind the row of houses, leading down to an old fashioned earth closet at the bottom. He was walking out of the house when he ran face to face with the Dysons just coming in.

One can feel for the Dysons as they saw him. Approaching the house they had seen Bolsover, whom they knew to be Peace's creature, leaning against the street lamp outside. Dyson was shocked into silence, but the formidable Mrs. Dyson was of sterner stuff. She had walked up to Bolsover and asked what he wanted. A shrug of the shoulders and an insolent grin was the only response. Turning to enter the house—their supposedly safe refuge—they found the dreaded ex-convict grinning evilly into their faces.

"You see," he sneered, "I'm here to annoy you, wherever you go," following this up with a series of obscene jibes.

Dyson pushed past him into the house, with face averted, doing his best to behave as though Peace was non-existent, but Catherine Dyson stood her ground. "There's a warrant out for you," she told him.

"I care nought for the warrant, nor for the bobbies," replied Peace coolly, but his actions belied his words. With a final oath he walked away into the night, followed by Bolsover. Mrs. Dyson stood on the doorstep and watched him go. Then she walked into the house and closed the door behind her. It no longer seemed much of a protection against the world. The fortress was breached. Throughout that evening, and the next and the next, Mr. Dyson kept anxious watch out of their windows for the familiar figure with the peculiarly distinctive gait, but there were no signs of Peace.

Perhaps after all he had thought better of his threats.

Peace was not in Sheffield. He was in Manchester. He had gone there to attend the trial, which opened on November 27th, of the two Habron brothers for the murder of P.C. Cock. He was to sit in the Public Gallery throughout the proceedings, which lasted two days, and he early won the attentive admiration of his neighbours in the Gallery for his expert knowledge of the points of law raised. He gave something of a running commentary of what was going forward.

In view of the outcome of the trial and its sequel it is only fair to observe that the trial was conducted by Mr. Justice Lindley, of whom Mr. W. T. Shore, who wrote the *Trials of Charles Frederick Peace* in the "Notable British Trials" series, commented that he was newly appointed and had little experience of criminal trials.

The Prosecuting Counsel, Mr. W. H. Higgins, Q.C., said that Cock had charged the two Habrons in the dock with being drunk and disorderly and on July 27th William had been fined 5s. and costs. The case against John had been adjourned until August 1, the morning before Cock died, when it had been dismissed by the Magistrate.

A parade of witnesses was called to say that around this time the Habrons had uttered threats against Cock. Abraham Wilcox, a local watchmaker, recounted that John had said of Cock: "If he does anything to me, or either of my brothers, by God I'll shoot him." He had been so impressed by the vehemence of Habron's tone he had taken it upon himself to warn Cock and also Cock's mother.

Mrs. Eleanor Carter, of the Royal Oak Public House, which was used regularly by the Habrons, said that John had told her if the "little bobby" summoned him "I'll make it hot for him. We'll shunt the bugger". She had then said: "Tha'll what, Jack?" and Habron had replied: "We'll get our gaffer to shift him. He is not the first he has shifted and he will shift him".

James Brownhill, a local wheelwright, said that on one occasion in his shop John Habron had said that one or other of his brothers would "shoot the bugger", meaning Cock. He personally hadn't thought much of it. He thought it was talk.

There was a curious piece of evidence given by two women. Sarah Beck Fox, of Chorlton, said that after the first police court hearing on July 27th she had seen John and Frank Habron with a Miss Elizabeth Whitelegg, a laundress in the district, talking together. Miss Whitelegg asked John how he had got on. John had said his case had been adjourned until the Tuesday "and if he (meaning Cock) does me, I will do him before Wednesday".

Called to the witness stand in her turn Miss Whitelegg said that she remembered this conversation, but added that on August 1st, early in the afternoon, she had seen John and he had asked her how her young man was—the significance of this being that "the young man" was Cock. She had said he was all right.

The matter was not pursued further in court, though there was clearly an interesting point here. John Habron and Cock were of an age. Is it possible that there was some rivalry, possibly jealousy, over the laundress, Miss Whitelegg?

Whatever the background to the relationship it is surely an odd thing for a man who contemplates the slaughter of another to inquire of his victim's sweetheart about his victim's health. Nor does anybody seem to have paid much attention to the fact that, after all, John had got away with his case. Cock's charge against him had been dismissed. If anybody looked foolish it was Cock himself.

The Prosecution ground on with its case of circumstantial evidence. Simpson, the young law student, said that the day after the crime he had been called to Old Trafford Police Station and there seen a man he now knew to be William Habron, in a brown coat like the one worn by the man he had seen under the street lamp when talking to Cock and Beanland.

Yes, he said, the man he had seen was similar to William Habron in height and build. Then he added that he had thought the man he had seen under the lamp *was an elderly man from his stoop and general appearance.*

Beanland, the policeman, gave evidence in marked conflict to Simpson's. He had not seen a man until the conversation between himself, Cock and Simpson was concluded and Simpson walked away. Then he had seen a man, who had stopped *under the lamp* (an odd thing for an intending murderer by stealth to do on a dark night). He was sure this man was young and fresh-complexioned. "I could see well from the light of the gas." He admitted he could not swear that it was William Habron he had seen under the light.

Though it seemed clear that Cock must have seen his killer—for he had been shot at close range—both Police Constable Ewen and Police Sergeant Thompson agreed that though they had asked him several times Cock had said he did not know who had shot him. To Ewen he had said: "I do not know. They have done me."

To Thompson, in Dr. Dill's surgery, Cock had said: "Leave me a be. Oh, Frank, you are killing me," though there was no Frank in the room.

The star witness for the Prosecution was Superintendent Bent. He described how he had pushed his way into the hut where the Habrons were in bed. "The prisoners did not say a word. They did not seem like men who had been asleep. I pulled the clothes off them and told them to remain quiet; then made them get up one by one and dress.

"I told them to put their boots on, and when they had put their feet in their boots I asked them to return them to me. I kept William's boots and allowed the others to put their own on again. William's boots were wet and 'slutchy' (dirty or muddy). They appeared to have been recently wetted. The others appeared to have been recently wetted, but were not 'slutchy'. William put a top hat on.

"I handcuffed them. I had up to that time made no charge. I then said, 'Mind what I am about to say. You three men are charged with murdering Police Constable Cock.' That was all I said. I had named neither day, place nor time. Upon that John raised his hands and said, 'I was in bed at the time'. I had not mentioned any time. Frank and William did not speak."

Bent said he had searched the outhouse but had found no firearms. (In fact the police had raked over the entire district, dragging streams, draining dykes and examining every inch of the nurseries and the adjoining farm, but they never did find a firearm.)

In the outhouse he had found a candle on the mantelpiece, which was half burnt and soft as if it had just been blown out. He believed he had seen the light from this candle when he had first approached the outhouse, the light that had been quickly extinguished.

At daylight, the Superintendent added, he had gone to the scene of the murder. He had earlier posted officers to stop people walking about there. On the private road to Firs Farm, and consequently to the back part of the nurseries, he had found on sand gravel a footprint corresponding in every particular to William's left boot. He had made another impression with that boot near the first footprint, and the impressions had matched exactly. (The boot was handed to the judge, who examined it closely, and later to the jury.)

Superintendent Bent described to the Court in great detail the marks of the nails, worn patches and so forth on the boot and how they had corresponded with the imprint. A number of policemen, and two outside witnesses, whom the Superintendent had taken with him to the scene, were to give evidence that in their opinions the two bootprints matched.

Cross-examined by Mr. J. H. P. Leresche, Defending Counsel, Superintendent Bent admitted—and it was perhaps the most significant admission of the whole trial—"I suspected the three men from the first", but he denied that he had told them, as soon as he got into their home: "Get up, you men, you have killed Police Constable Cock."

The Prosecution were, however, able to prove that though William Habron and indeed all the Habrons had told Bent they were in bed by nine o'clock on the night of the murder, the two men on trial had been, in fact, drinking in local hotels until at least half-past ten, possibly until eleven.

A labourer, John Walsh, said that he had gone to call for the men early in the evening to go for a drink and when he did so William had his boots off to go to bed and had to be persuaded to go out again. By common consent it was agreed that Frank, the brother not on trial, had been in bed by 9.30.

The Prosecution now produced their most curious evidence. The first, Donald McClelland, an assistant in an ironmonger's shop three-and-a-half miles from Deakin's Nurseries, said that on July 31st, or August 1st—he couldn't remember which—a man he now identified as William Habron came to his shop and tried to buy some cartridges.

He had shown this man some cartridges and asked him if he had his revolver with him to test whether the cartridges would fit. (These were days when revolvers were rather haphazard in design.) The customer had hesitated, then said "No". He had shown the man a revolver that would take the cartridges, telling him it cost 35s., "but we have some cheaper for 10s." In the end the man had left the shop without making any purchase at all, either of pistol or cartridges.

Another assistant in the shop, John Henry Simpson, said he had been in the shop at the time, but he couldn't positively swear the man who had inquired about the cartridges was William. He thought he was, but couldn't be sure.

Apart from showing the somewhat startling ease with which revolvers could be bought in Victorian England, at a time when the Irish Republicans were extremely active, all these two shop assistants were saying was that a man had wanted to buy some cartridges, but hadn't.

The Defence called a number of witnesses to say that William could not have called at the ironmonger's shop at the time the two shopmen said the man had called for cartridges. They also produced witnesses to show that the Habrons were excellent workmen and regarded hitherto as men of good character, a fact which the Prosecution did not deny.

Summing up, Mr. Justice Lindley pointed out that the murder of P.C. Cock had caused a lot of excitement in Manchester: "The probability is you have heard through the newspapers a great deal more about it than I have."

Just before five o'clock on the second day the jury retired to consider their verdict. They were out two-and-a-half hours, before solemnly filing back to their places. Peace leaned forward eagerly. "They won't look at the chaps in the dock if it's guilty," he told those nearby; "they never does if it's guilty."

The jury's verdict was read out. William was "Guilty", John "Not Guilty". The Foreman added that the jury wished to add a recommendation to mercy for William because of his youth.

William was asked if he had anything to say. He replied, "I am innocent." Then the Judge donned the black cap and said: "You have been found guilty by the jury of murdering P.C. Cock. It is my duty to pass sentence upon you. The trial has been long, but not unnecessarily so for the evidence which had to be adduced against you consisted of a number of small details, which had to be proved and all of which had to be carefully considered together. The Jury most patiently listened to the whole and they found the verdict they have just found. I shall simply discharge my duty by passing the sentence of death upon you. It will be my duty to present to Her Majesty's Government the recommendation to mercy which the Jury have made by reason of your youth, but having regard to the fact that you have been found guilty you must not be deceived—for the murder which is now found to have been a murder committed by yourself was a cruel murder—and you must not be surprised if that recommendation is disregarded. However that does not rest with me, but with Her Majesty's Government.

"The sentence is that you be taken from this place to the place whence you came and thence to a place of execution and that you be there hanged by the neck until you are dead and that your body be afterwards buried in the precincts of the gaol wherein you were last confined before the execution of this judgement upon you. And may the Lord have mercy upon your soul."

Hardly had the Chaplain intoned his customary amen before the warders began to hustle Habron from the dock—they usually do this, nothing unseemly must happen to disturb a judge—but before he disappeared he raised his hands and shouted: "I am innocent."

Mr. Justice Lindley's attitude appears to have been one of rare emotional detachment, even for a British judge at a murder trial. They usually manage to preserve a serene detachment that persuades themselves, if nobody else, that they are personally not involved, while earning a large salary, in the killing of another man, if he be found guilty.

But Mr. Justice Lindley's reactions were even more serenely awful than usual. It was strikingly obvious that he was not too happy about the verdict. It was noticeable that he made none of the usual references to the jury's verdict being the correct one, yet he calmly assured Habron that his hopes of a reprieve were slender once he had been found guilty. Indeed they were. There was no Court of Criminal Appeal then. This verdict was final. A reprieve was the only hope, and killers of policemen cannot expect much in the way of mercy from the Government.

Charles Peace went back to his lodgings. Mr. A. F. Williams, of Manchester, says that during the trial Peace and a woman stayed, under the alias of Mr. and Mrs. Robinson, with his grandmother, who had just been left a widow with two young boys. Peace, he reports, "came home very upset and when my grandmother asked him how the case had gone he said 'They have sentenced him to death. The police have sworn his life away. He is no more guilty than you are Mrs. Williams . . .'

"In the bedroom which he occupied was a chest of drawers, and he asked if he could have the use of one of the drawers as Mrs. Robinson had a dress which was spoiling in the trunk so that he was given the use of one drawer, the others being locked, but this one drawer gave him access to the drawer underneath in which was my grandfather's last best suit. When he left after the case was over he walked out in the suit he had stolen."

Though Mr. Peace was not satisfied with the verdict, the Manchester public were glad to feel that British justice had triumphed once again. One Manchester newspaper devoted a leader to the trial the next morning. "The Jury's verdict was accompanied by a strong recommendation to mercy on the grounds of the convict's youth. The recommendation will, of course, receive due consideration in the proper quarter, but it is difficult to discover mitigating circumstances in this case. The crime was planned with cool deliberation and executed with reckless daring. We imagine that few persons will be found to dispute the justice of the conclusion which has been reached."

One can almost feel even now the self-satisfaction that

accompanied the penning of this leader, and the sage man-of-the-world nodding of heads which took place over the breakfast tables in the city the next morning. Fortunately there were those who kept cooler heads and were profoundly unhappy about the verdict. A petition was got up and forwarded to the Government for a reprieve. But the days went by and there was no sign of any movement at Whitehall.

In the awful seclusion of the death cell William Habron, the illiterate 18-year-old labourer, bore himself with dignity and courage. He formed a deep bond with the Roman Catholic Father who attended him, Father Corbishley, and convinced him—and indeed even the hard-bitten prison officials—that he was an innocent man. Not that, one fears, this would have stayed their hand in assisting him to the gallows.

Habron insisted that the police had not seen a light put out as they had approached the outhouse on the night of the murder. He told Father Corbishley: "The police must have been mistaken. They approached from different sides of the hut and I think one policeman must have seen the gleaming light of another policeman's lantern and thought it was a light from the hut."

The Home Office does not normally divulge how it adjudicates in deciding to reprieve, or not reprieve, a condemned man. Ultimately the decision, of course, is the Home Secretary's, but it is probable that the actual decision is shuffled off by being passed around a select group of people called upon to give an opinion. It is likely that the trial judge is asked to give an opinion, and indeed, if this is so, no doubt his opinion is given great weight; though why judges, usually drawn from a very narrow segment of society, should be considered able to weigh up the moral dilemmas of men from other walks of society is hard to guess. One wonders, for example, how an ex-public schoolboy, who has passed through the channel of Christ Church, Oxford, to eminence and wealth at the Bar can understand, say, the motives of an illegitimate girl, raised to whoredom in the gutters of a seaport, in knocking a faithless lover on the head. However, the decision was reached thirty-six hours before the dutiful men of the prison service would have walked out a man they believed to be innocent and hung him. Habron was reprieved. He passed out of sight into the obscurity of the convict prisons and would in the ordinary course of events have rotted away for fifteen or twenty years. In fact he was to serve only two years . . .

When the reprieve came through Habron was at first elated, but within a few days he became restless and began to complain that he should be released. On the morning that he was due to have died, a man called Flanagan was executed in the same prison. Habron told Father Corbishley: "Well, it is all over for him and would have been all over for me, too. Now I shall perhaps be in prison all the days of my life, but as long as I live I shall always pray they will find the man who killed Cock."

It was in 1879 when he was labouring in the bleak quarries of Portland Prison that his prayer was answered.

Early in 1879 Peace was in the condemned cell himself awaiting execution for another crime. He asked that the Rev. Littlewood, the Vicar of Darnall, might come to see him. "I can tell that man anything," he said. The authorities agreed, hoping that Peace would tell the Vicar the secret of his disposal of stolen goods.

It was true that the Vicar was to hear a confession. Peace poured out hundreds of words and, after dealing with certain other matters told the Vicar:—

"I was in Manchester in 1876 and I was there to 'work' some houses. I went to a place called Whalley Range. I had 'spotted' a house there which I thought I could get into without much trouble . . .

"On my way to the house that night I passed two policemen on the road. I may tell you I did not go to any house by accident. I always went some days, sometimes weeks before, carefully examining all the surroundings and then, having spotted a 'likely' house, I studied the neighbourhood, both as to the means of getting in and as to getting away.

"There were some grounds about that house, and my object was to get into these grounds in the dark, and wait a convenient time for getting into the house.

"I missed the policemen, and for a moment I thought they had not suspected me, and had not come my way. I must have been mistaken. I walked into the grounds through the gate, and before I was able to begin to 'work' I heard a rustling and a step behind me. Looking back I saw a policeman, whose figure was the same as one of the two I passed on the road, coming into the grounds. He had evidently seen me turn back and followed.

"I saw I could do no work that night, and then doubled to elude him. For a moment I succeeded, and taking a favourable chance, I endeavoured to make my escape. As quickly as I could I jumped on the wall and, as I was dropping down and had cleared the premises, I almost fell into the arms of the second policeman, who must have been planted in the expectation that I would escape that way.

"This policeman—I did not know his name—made a grab at me. My blood was up, because I was nettled that I had been disturbed, having 'spotted' that house for a long time and determined to do it—so I told him, 'You stand back, or I'll shoot you.'

"He didn't stand back, but came on, and I stepped back a few yards and fired wide at him, purposely to frighten him that I might get away.

"And now, Sir, I want to tell you, and I want you to believe me, that I always made it a rule during the whole of my career never to take life if I could avoid it."

The convict said this very earnestly, and looked at Mr. Littlewood as if he expected a further reassurance of his faith in him on that score. "Yes, Sir, whether you believe me or not I never wanted to take human life. I never wanted to murder anybody. I only wanted to do what I came to do and get away, but it does seem odd, after all, that in the end I should have to be hanged for having taken life—the very thing I always endeavoured to avoid. I have never willingly or knowingly, hurt a living creature. I would not even hurt an animal, much less a man.

"That is why I tell you, Sir, that I fired wide on him, but the policeman, like most Manchester policemen, was a determined man. They are a very obstinate lot, these Manchester policemen. He was no doubt as determined as I was myself and you know that when I am put to it, I can do that which very few men can do.

"After I fired wide of him—and it was all the work of a few

moments, Sir—I noticed that he had seized his staff, which was in his pocket, and was rushing at me and about to strike me. I saw I had no time to lose if I wanted to get away at all that night. I then fired the second time, and I assure you again that then I had no intention of killing him. All I wanted to do was to disable the arm which carried the staff, in order that I might get away. But instead of that he came on to seize me and we had a scuffle together. I could not take as careful an aim as I would have done and the bullet missed the arm, struck him in the breast and he fell. I know no more. I got away, which was all I wanted.

"I left Manchester and went to Hull. Some time afterwards I saw it announced in the papers that certain men had been taken into custody for the murder of this policeman. This greatly interested me. I always had a liking to be present at trials, as the public no doubt knew by this time, and I determined to be present at this trial. I left Hull for Manchester, not telling my family where I had gone, and attended the Assizes at Manchester for two days and heard the youngest of the brothers, as I was told they were, sentenced to death . . .

"Now, Sir, some people will say that I was a hardened wretch for allowing an innocent man to suffer for my guilt, for the crime of which I was guilty, but what man would have given himself up under such circumstances, knowing, as I did, that I should certainly be hanged for the crime?

"But now that I am going to forfeit my own life, and feel that I have nothing to gain by further secrecy, I think it is right in the sight of God and man to clear this young man, who is entirely innocent of the crime."

Peace then went on with other events, but persuaded by the Vicar, and the Governor of the prison in which he was confined, he agreed to write out his own version of the affair for forwarding to the Home Office. He was asked to point out any further details he could remember about the crime.

He wrote:—

"This is the confession of Charles Peace now under sentence of death now in H.M. Prison, Leeds:—

"On the 27 and 28 of nov 1876 at Manchester assizes thare was tow brothers triad for the murder of Police man Cox in Seymour Grove at Whalley Range near Manchester ther was from seven to ten witnesses appeared against them and all of them but one perjered themselves against them to the uttermost for I saw the trial myself and the only person that spoke the truth was a civilian not the lawyer's son for he did not speak the truth.

"The circumstances of the case are as follows:—

"On tuesday night the 1st of August 1876 aboute Midnight I was at Brookes Bar and you will see by the word me on the Plan (Peace drew a plan of the scene) that I went from Brookes Bar to Seymour Grove and as I turned the corner of Seymour Grove I saw the Police men and two civilians stood at the 'ducking stone' (he meant 'jutting') I crossed the road and went up Seymour Grove and then into the grounds of the third house as shown on the plan one of the Police men followed me there and stude on the steps of the house with his bulls eye on and I came over the wall into Seymour Grove and crossed the road to where (me) is marked (on the Plan) and then saw a Police man crossing the road from the corner (more details of the drawn plan followed) towards me and I saw his intention and fired off one chamber of my revolver for to frighten him but he still came forward to within a yard and a half of myself I discharged another chamber and the Ball which struck him on the nipple of the right breast and then he threw up his walking stick saying Ah you bugger and then fell and I turned round and crossed over into the grounds of the fourth house I then made good my escape by climbing over the wall at the back of the house crossing the lane and then to Old Trafford railway station and went through the tunnell and walked on the line for about two miles before I took the road as I crossed the fields I saw a man working by a fire near the railway but who did not see me

"As I was in the act of making my escape over the wall of the fourth house I heard a dog barking

"The two brothers who were charged with This murder were named Frank and Aaron Harman. Frank was acquitted and Aaron sentenced to death but recommended to mercy on account of his youth and after wards repreved by the Secretary of State down to life. as prooff of his innocence you will find that the ball that was taken out of Cox's breast is one of the Heley No 9 pinfire cartridges and was fired out of my revolver now at leeds town hall and if you take the ball out of one of the Heley No 9 pinfire cartidge it and the one taken out of cox's body both will weight alike and allso bouth of them to fit into one cartridge case what I have said is nothing but the truth and this man is inosence."

He concluded with a flourish of moral rectitude: "I have done my duty and leve the rest to you."

This document was passed to the Home Office and then to the Chief Constable of Lancashire, the Honourable Captain Legge, for the matter to be investigated. On February 23rd, 1879, Captain Legge reported to the Home Secretary:—

"I yesterday visited the place where Police Constable Cock was murdered on 1st August, 1876, and have endeavoured to sift the truth of Peace's statement. With regard to the plan of the locality drawn by him I have to inform you that it is substantially correct, though several inaccuracies exist in it, and is such a plan as a burglar well acquainted with the district, as Peace has been for a long time, having been twice convicted of burglaries committed in the neighbourhood in the years 1859 and 1866, might easily have drawn.

"As regards his account of what occurred on the night in question, I would observe that it corresponds in great measure with the evidence given at the trial of the brothers Habron, but he is incorrect in saying there were 'two civilians' standing with the two constables at the 'ducking' (this should be 'jutting') stone when the man, who crossed from Whalley Range over Seymour Grove into the garden of a house on the other side of the latter road, came up. The witness Simpson was the only one there at all that night and he had left the constables and gone in the direction of Brooks Bar before the man, whom P.C. Beanland followed, did so . . . (Captain Legge here went into details of the plan drawn by Peace, pointing out certain discrepancies) . . .

"I have *pressed* (this word underlined by the Chief Constable) Constable Beanland very closely on this point and can have no doubt that he is correct; and this Constable also says he does not believe it possible for a man to have made his escape in the direction indicated by Peace without him seeing him as it took less time for him to reach the gate from Gratrix's doorstep, where he was standing when the shots were fired, than it would for a man to have got out of sight going as Peace says he did . . ."

The Chief Constable here referred to the plan again and added that Peace had not included in his plan a road between two houses and had missed out details of the buildings he would have had to pass to reach the open fields to escape.

"It is true, however, that men were working day and night at a sewer in those fields and had a fire burning at the time. It also appears that Peace and William Habron are about the same size, the former being described in our books at 5 feet 3½ inches tall in 1859 and 5 feet 4 inches tall in 1866, and the latter as 5 feet 3½ inches tall. Beyond this their descriptions do not agree, but I think the evidence on that point at Habron's trial was not very conclusive.

"I propose to take the bullet found in Cock's body to Leeds tomorrow with a view to ascertaining if it could, or is likely, to have been fired from Peace's pistol and will report the result."

The Chief Constable then suggested there were certain questions he might put to Peace about the houses in Seymour Grove that would help to establish the truth and he asked the Home Secretary to telegraph instructions to the Governor of the Prison at Leeds to grant him permission to see the convict. There is now no record of whether these questions were put to Peace and, if so, what his replies were. Indeed the Home Secretary forbade the Chief Constable to question Peace personally, ordering that any questions be put through the Governor of the Prison.

It was a very fair report, indeed exceptionally so when one considers that Captain Legge was himself, in the final analysis, the man who had prosecuted the Habrons and could not like to think he had participated in a dreadful miscarriage of justice. It is difficult not to feel admiration for Captain Legge's conclusions in his report.

"There was much that occurred at the time of the murder that could not be made evidence which seemed to fasten the guilt on one or more of the Habrons, but it seems difficult to perceive what motive Peace can have in charging himself with it unless he was really the perpetrator of it."

The Honourable Captain Legge was, in truth, an honourable man.

His concluding argument is a powerful one. Peace was maintaining that the crime for which he had been condemned to death was another of his "accidental" killings. There was no reason for him to damn his faintest chance of a reprieve by admitting another murder.

Mistakes in his plan are not surprising. Peace had burgled many houses and had many narrow escapes in his life. It is not unlikely he confused certain details of the locale with other events in other places. It is significant that the human details, the slinking past the workmen with the fire in the dark and the matter of the barking dog (a worrying sound for a burglar), give his confession the ring of truth. On the professional details he could not be faulted.

Though the science of ballistics was then in its infancy the experts agreed that the bullet taken from Cock's body was fired from a pistol of the type taken from Peace. One witness insisted that it could be stated that without doubt the ball came from Peace's pistol.

At first the Home Office—and some newspapers—were reluctant to accept Peace's story. No one cared to think that the Law had made such an appalling mistake as to sentence a boy of 18 to death for a crime he had not committed. However, Habron was removed from the harsh discipline of penal life and placed in the prison hospital while the experts at the Home Office considered what they were going to do.

The Rev. Littlewood, in a letter to the *Manchester Guardian* which took a sceptical view of Peace's confession, wrote:—"Whether Police Constable Cock did use, or was about to use, a staff or stick is of no importance whatever, the result was the same to the brave and faithful officer, his life having been sacrificed.

"On the second point, that of the scuffle, there is strong presumptive evidence that my memory did not mislead me. If there was no scuffle why did Peace cry out, 'You stand back, or I'll shoot you'. Then, is it likely that after the first shot was fired, the resolute policeman would stand perfectly still as a post and not make any attempt to defend himself, or capture his deadly foe? I am fully persuaded in my own mind that Charles Peace was the murderer of Police Constable Cock."

There were people who said that Peace had made his confession to obtain a postponement of his execution. The Rev. Osmond Cookson, Chaplain of Armley Prison, Leeds, said later that the idea was quite false. Peace, he said, knew he must die.

Finally Authority agreed to admit a mistake had been made. Some months later, long after Peace himself had been executed, Habron was granted a free pardon and an indemnity of £800: not a large sum though, of course, far more then than it seems today. It was little enough recompense even so for the ordeal of lying under sentence of death for weeks, and enduring the horrors of Victorian penal establishments.

It is a sobering thought that today it would be unthinkable for the State to reprieve a man convicted of murdering a policeman, whatever the circumstances. Today Habron would have been executed. One wonders, too, in view of recent cases whether after once executing a man the Home Office would admit it had made this irreversible mistake. Victorian Justice did not set the policeman above ordinary members of the public as a class apart for special protection.

Just after Cock was shot the local residents of Chorlton-cum-Hardy and Old Trafford, local magistrates and other policemen subscribed to the cost of a memorial stone for the grave in the churchyard of St. Clements, Chorlton-cum-Hardy. Later it was brought to the grounds of the headquarters of the Lancashire Constabulary.

It reads:

To the Memory of Nicholas Cock.

An Able and Energetic Officer of the County Constabulary who on 2nd August 1876 while engaged in the faithful discharge of his duty was cruelly assassinated.

This monument was raised by voluntary contributions; the subscribers consisting of Magistrates, The Officers and Men of his own Force and citizens in general who felt that some public tribute was due to the name of one who while in his private capacity deserved well of those who knew him, for zeal and fidelity in his office was worthy of honoured remembrance by all.

Aged 20 years
Be Thou Faithful unto Death
and He will give Thee a crown of life.

It is a sad memorial to one who died on the threshold of life. It is also a salutary reminder to all of us that we owe much to the men who are prepared to risk their lives to protect us from the rapacity of criminals.

Many years afterwards the man who was in many ways the key figure in the Habron trial, Police Superintendent Bent, wrote of the case in a way that throws more light on how the Habrons came to find themselves in the predicament they did.

Bent was almost as classically a Victorian personality as Peace. He was, in many ways, typical of the very best type of English policeman, imbued with "Cop's Honour", resolute and zealous in his duty, but without animus against the men he sought. He had a warm heart and many endearing qualities of personality. He was religious in the old austere manner, yet without any sense of moral superiority towards men of weaker calibre. His appearance was highly impressive; he was stocky, with a flowing beard and a level penetrating gaze. Indeed his probing glance was so steely and menacing to the wrongdoer that he used it as a weapon to break down the defences of hardened criminals. On one occasion he saw a man behaving suspiciously near a large house, but had no pretext to arrest him. He gazed at the man steadily, until unnerved by this unblinking hostility the suspect made a run for it. Bent caught up with him and, without further questioning, the man blurted out a confession of robbery.

Nonetheless it was this frightening thief-taker, who at a time when most of his contemporaries saw unmoved the awful spectacle of poverty about them, organised and ran, with the aid of his wife, a soup kitchen alleviating the distress of thousands of starving children.

His courage was proverbial. He bore to his old age the scars—and recurrent pains—of fearful injuries sustained in a desperate battle to arrest a criminal of large physique and ferocity whom Bent pursued alone into the criminal quarter of the city. He held his man despite a rain of blows from a heavy bludgeon.

It is endearing in a man of Bent's proven courage to have his own admission that he liked reading cheap blood and thunder novelettes, but, if he read them when Mrs. Bent was out of the house, he would leave the door open because the more bloodthirsty pages would bring him out in a cold sweat. It is an amusing confession for a man who would tackle men who would kill him if they could and who plunged first into a house containing three men he believed would shoot rather than be taken alive.

One cannot blame Bent for believing the Habrons to be guilty of shooting Cock. He had every reason to do so. Cock had told him: "Mr. Bent, I know these men very well. They have threatened several times to shoot me within the last few months if ever I summoned them." Bent records that the morning the summons against John was dismissed Cock came to him and said: "Mr. Bent, John Habron has just told me he will shoot me before 12 p.m. tonight". What else could Bent think when at about that time he was told that Cock had, in fact, been shot?

The Habrons, too, certainly did not help themselves. Bent recorded: "At the Police Station all three prisoners were seen separately and they all said one after another that they were in bed the previous night at nine, though I found this to be untrue because they had been drinking at a public house, near the outbuildings, until nearly 11 o'clock. Cock would have passed this Public House at about 5 to 11 to walk to West Point (where he was killed)."

Bent received a number of threatening letters during the Habron trial and adds: "After the liberation of John I had grave doubts concerning his attitude towards several witnesses in the case. I considered it my duty to tell him I have received so many complaints about his conduct and threatening people's lives that if any person, who had given evidence in the case, received an injury I should hold him responsible and would find him if he went to the other end of the world." No more was heard of threats to witnesses.

When William was released Bent bore no malice. He wrote: "I do not hesitate for one moment to say that when the time arrived at which William was discharged from jail he had not a friend in the world more pleased to hear of his release than I was and he came to see me at my house several times. No man felt more grieved than I did when I heard of William Habron's subsequent troubles. I believe he would have done anything in his power that I wished him to do."

No, Superintendent Bent cannot be held responsible. Society uses the Bents for their courage and their zeal, but they do have the faults of their virtues. They hang on like bulldogs, even when sometimes they are wrong. They cannot easily be swayed from a quarry once their hunter's blood is up. It is a good thing for all of us that they cannot. Bent believed the Habrons to be guilty; it was his duty—and his nature—to pursue them to the execution shed, even though he appears to have disliked capital punishment.

The outstanding mystery of the night Cock died is the curious conflict of evidence between Simpson, the law student, and Beanland, the policeman. Why did both see a man at a time when the other did not? Were there perhaps two men about near that junction of roads that night? There is evidence of a woman living in a turning off the private road to the Firs Farm, that she—and her husband—the night of the murder heard the noise of something, or somebody, running fast across the road and towards the ditches that lead round to Deakin's Nurseries.

In this context there is Captain Legge's statement that certain evidence existed which could not be brought forward in court, pointing to the guilt of the Habrons. A report in the *Manchester Guardian* on February 21, 1879, tended to throw cold water on Peace's confession and put up the suggestion that three men were engaged that night in a conspiracy to get at Cock, but had no quarrel with Beanland.

Said the Guardian's reporter, "If, as we are strongly disposed to do, we dismiss Peace altogether from the scene, we may account for the presence of the two men who were seen to come up Upper Chorlton Road in this way . . . a conspiracy had been laid to murder Cock, but the conspirators had no grudge against Beanland. Hence by an ingenious stratagem they contrived to detach Beanland from his companion. The two men were successful in their purpose, a third, whoever he may be, approaching Cock as he stood by the wall and shooting him down."

Reporters normally seek their information from police officers in situations of this kind. It is possible, then, that the *Guardian* reporter was passing on a view the police formed from evidence they could not produce in court. Is it possible that one, or two, of the Habrons had hoped that night to waylay Cock and knock him about as a means of paying off old scores? They had been drinking and their tempers were inflamed. Were they dissuaded from this purpose by finding that Cock was accompanied by Beanland and Simpson? If so, their position when Cock was killed was extremely hazardous and they could only keep quiet, strong Irish family loyalty keeping their tongues sealed.

There can certainly be no question that the jury ought not to have convicted William Habron. The evidence before them was woefully thin, but prejudices at that time were strong. Both Manchester and nearby Liverpool had large Irish populations. They were not popular. These were times when religious differences were keen and the Roman Catholicism of the Irish was regarded with distaste by the bulk of the populace. There was also the aggravation of the shootings and murders brought about by the Irish struggle for political independence. In Manchester itself, some years before the Habron trial, there was a pitched battle involving scores of men, when Irish Republicans sought to rescue two of their kind from a police wagon *en route* to jail. A British Police Sergeant, inside the wagon, was gunned down and later a number of the captured Irishmen were executed.

At such times it could be that illiterate Irishmen, when swearing vengeance, would talk of "shooting" and that English jurymen would see in every Irishman a representative of the desperate gunmen of the Irish Republican movement.

One section of public opinion had no doubts about William Habron's innocence. The criminal community of Manchester and Sheffield had heard the rumours that Peace had boasted to certain confidantes that he had "done for" a young policeman who had interfered with him at Whalley Range.

There is another aspect of the Habron trial which gives it unique interest, and that is Peace's reaction as he walked away from the Manchester Assize Court after hearing William Habron sentenced to death. What he was about to do was a startling illustration of the fact that the origins of crime in the individual are deeper and more complex than most people suspect. It is easy to realise, in theory, that the cruel death of hanging—mostly a slow and painful business despite the contrary myth that has grown up—inflicted in cold blood in retribution for deeds almost invariably committed in passion or in mental derangement, is useless except as a palliative to the general public. It is logical to think that only a deranged mind would contemplate risking its own life by committing murder, for almost invariably the gains from murder are either illusory, as in crimes of passion, or trumpery, in the cases of killing for gain.

It is easy to accept all this rationally, but such is the difficulty in allying reason with the instinctive assessments of training and environment, that Peace's actions after the Habron trial are still startling.

For the day after watching a man sentenced to death for a crime he had committed himself Peace was to shoot down another man. The Great Deterrent to murder—as the supporters of Capital Punishment speak of judicial killing—did not deter him.

CHAPTER FOUR

The next day Peace was back in Sheffield. He had gone to attend the Winter Fair, but, so far as is known, he never got to it—which no doubt meant that quite a few revellers got home with their purses intact, for he never altogether gave up his first criminal trade of picking pockets. In the early afternoon he went into a public house in Ecclesall Road. By mid-afternoon he had drunk more than his accustomed ration. The excitement of the Habron trial, the tension of being a hunted man in his own city, his obsession with Mrs. Dyson, combined with the potent brews to turn his brain into something like manic over-activity. Everything in that strange mind was swirling round in a positive explosion of energy, alternating with the rapidity of a short circuit between geniality and fury.

He forced conversations on strangers, insisted on pouring out his venom against "that whore", pulling out packets of letters and photographs from his pockets to prove the points of his rambling tale of a woman's treachery and his hatred of her husband. Then, in a moment, he was singing or dancing a jig, for the taproom was full and there was singing and a general air of alcoholic holiday bonhomie.

" 'Ere, I'll give you a tune," he told the company. "I'll show you something no other man in England can do." He manufactured a strange musical instrument with a piece of long string, a poker and a short stick. He tautened the string almost to breaking-point by hanging the heavy poker on it, then began to strum the airs of a jig on it with the stick. Soon the company were dancing to the beat of this bizarre contrivance as its even more bizarre musician stood wielding his stick with a mounting fury, as more and more drinks were passed up to him.

The afternoon wore on towards the early dusk of November, faster and faster went the beat of the music, wilder and wilder became the dancing as the smoky taproom became an inferno of drunken men and women. Under the impact of his own music and the drink all the restraints of caution began to break down in Peace's mind. How dare the Dysons laugh at him? He'd show them. The man who'd fooled all the police in England, who knew things about that murder of a policeman in Manchester no other living soul knew—or ever would know. How he hated that woman—no, not her so much. At least once she had admitted his attraction, until that mealy-mouthed middle-class beanpole of a husband had turned her against him. Dyson! How he wished he could get at his throat now . . . .

In the middle of a tune Peace turned away, threw down his stick and lurched into the dusk. Nobody did what Dyson had done to Charlie Peace and boasted of it.

The Rev. E. Newman, Vicar of Ecclesall, was just sitting down to his tea when his maid told him that there was a strange "person" without who insisted on speaking to him. It was Peace, who launched into a tirade to the astonished Vicar about the Dysons. He had come, he said, to put the reverend gentleman "on his guard" against such a wicked couple. He had been carrying on an affair with Mrs. Dyson and offered to show proof of his allegations. "I was righteous until Mr. Dyson became jealous. Then I said to Mrs. Dyson we had better give Mr. Dyson something to talk about."

It was curious tit-for-tat morality even for Peace, to seduce a man's wife because that man is ignobly jealous of you, but Peace ranted on, saying that Mrs. Dyson taking out the summons against him had ruined his existence, spoiled his home life, destroyed his business and so on, until the poor Vicar's head was spinning. Still the flood of words poured out. He had forgiven Mrs. Dyson, he went on, but he could not forgive that wicked man, Mr. Dyson.

The unhappy Mr. Newman did his best to soothe his wild-eyed visitor. At twenty minutes to seven Mr. Newman ushered Peace out of his study after persuading him not to go near the Dysons that night. Peace promised that he wouldn't and left with a cheery "Good night."

With a sigh of relief the Vicar went back to his study. He felt he had accomplished some good that afternoon. It was true that Peace was at least normal as he trudged away from the Vicarage.

He thought he might just call in and see the Gregorys in their shop at Banner Cross. Then his thoughts began to turn from the Gregorys back towards their neighbours, the Dysons. Anger, wounded pride and hatred mounted in him once more. By the time he had walked to the Gregorys his brain was like a red-hot cinder again.

He found Mrs. Gregory in charge; she said her husband had gone out. Peace did not waste time with her. He left almost immediately. Mrs. Gregory felt somewhat uneasy. Neither she nor her husband had cared much for this strange little man with the bushy whiskers. She rather wished her husband would come home. She went to the door to look for him and to her dismay saw Peace creeping stealthily out of the entrance to the back-yards of the Banner Cross houses. He had obviously been lurking at the back of the Dysons' home.

Mrs. Gregory was relieved to see Peace shuffle off into the darkness towards Sheffield. He must have thought better of whatever he had intended and gone away, she told herself.

About half past seven Mrs. Sarah Colgreaves, the wife of a knife maker, living in Dobbin Hill, a little way from Banner Cross, decided to walk down to the Gregorys' for some late shopping. It was a pleasant moonlit night and as she walked along towards the shop, she saw a small man with a beard walking to and fro in the roadway. As she went by, this man asked her if she knew who lived in "that house," pointing to the one next door to the Gregorys. No, she did not, but believed them to be strangers.

"That woman is my bloody whore," was the response.

Mrs. Colgreaves was not having that. Tartly she told the man: "You ought to mind what you say".

Peace ignored this. "Would you mind going to the door and saying that an elderly gentleman wishes to see her?"

Mrs. Colgreaves said she minded very much. He had better run his own errands. With a shrug of impatience Peace turned away.

Inside the shop Mrs. Colgreaves found a somewhat agitated Mrs. Gregory who asked her if she had seen an elderly man creeping about. Mrs. Colgreaves told her what had happened and advised Mrs. Gregory to lock her door "with a man like that about". After she had left the shop she heard Mrs. Gregory turn the key in the lock. Looking round she again saw Peace. He was coming out of the entrance to the backyard. Seeing Mrs. Colgraves looking at him he made off, up the hill towards Ecclesall.

About eight a labourer, Charles Brassington, walked past the Banner Cross Hotel. He noticed, in the light of a street-lamp, a small, elderly man walking quickly to and fro on the pavement opposite the hotel. This man walked up to him and Brassington could see he was labouring under some strong emotion, his features working with passion. Did he know of any strangers living hereabouts, the odd little man asked him? No, he did not.

Peace, for it was Peace, then seized his arm and insisted that he look at a photograph. Brassington could see it was of a man and a woman. Embarrassed by all this Brassington tried to walk away, but Peace kept up with him and, at the next street-lamp, thrust a bundle of papers into his hands and asked him to read them. Brassington said he could not read.

Peace wasn't listening. "I will make it warm for them before morning. I'll shoot 'em both," then abruptly he broke away from Brassington and walked quickly across the road towards Gregory's shop.

Mrs. Gregory was still waiting behind her locked doors for her husband to come home. Where *was* the man, with that dreadful creature prowling about outside? Just about eight she heard the sound of clogs walking down the backyard towards the closet at the bottom. Mrs. Gregory peered out of her kitchen window. It was Mrs. Dyson, small lantern in hand . . .

Inside his home Mr. Dyson was sitting reading a book. This quiet man with pretensions to gentility had now only a few moments left to live. He had presented an unhappy, even undignified figure in the maelstrom of passion that two stronger characters had created. He yet had time to redeem himself as a man—and die for it.

Still hovering in her kitchen Mrs. Gregory heard a loud scream from the backyard. It was a woman's voice. She knew who had screamed and could guess something of the reason why. She opened her back door—a brave thing for a woman alone to do. The yard was a black pit.

At the same moment Dyson appeared at his back door. Mrs. Gregory told him: "Mr. Dyson, go to your wife". Without hesitation, the gigantic engineer walked quickly down into the darkness, though he must have guessed that a dangerous criminal lurked there who entertained for him an almost insane hatred.

Peace knew that once the woman had screamed he must get away—and quickly. He was trapped in that backyard with only one exit. As the huge figure of Dyson loomed above him he tore from his pocket the pistol he had used to slay P.C. Cock. The roar of the gun was like that of a cannon in the confined space. A bullet slammed against the wall. Peace dived for the road. Again his pistol flashed. Arthur Dyson slumped to the cobbles. Mrs. Dyson went on her knees beside him and cradled his head in her arms. She dabbed ineffectually at the blood oozing from the wound in the left temple. A strange, disjointed flow of words came from the gaping mouth.

Seventeen-year-old Thomas Wilson was standing in the roadway near Banner Cross when he heard the sound of the shots. There was a cloud across the moon and a light drizzle was falling, but he saw a man run across the road from the terrace houses, leap for the top of the wall at the other side and swing over like a giant monkey to disappear in the darkness of the fields beyond.

The noise of the shots had roused the neighbourhood; men ran into the courtyard and helped to carry Dyson back into his own sitting-room. They put him back in his chair and Mrs. Dyson bathed his face until Dr. Harrison, from nearby Cemetery Road, came in. On his orders Dyson was laid on a mattress on the floor and the doctor, Mrs. Dyson and Mrs. Gregory waited silently in the room. The only sound was the gabble of words coming from Dyson. When these ceased there was nothing except the ticking of the clock. It stood at a quarter to eleven, when the watchers heard Dyson's breathing stop for ever.

While Dyson was being carried into his home Police Constable Sylvester had arrived. A few quick questions told him what had happened. Today a constable would make a telephone call to headquarters and a team of highly mobile policemen would start combing the area for the fugitive gunman. Then, all P.C. Sylvester could do was walk stolidly for twenty minutes down the road to Highfield Police Station to report the killing. Inspector Jacob Bradbury returned by cab to the Dysons. By half past ten he knew the fugitive was Peace, with whom he was already well acquainted. Bradbury and a team of constables searched the city for Peace, but he had had over two hours' start—a long time for a man of Peace's background and experience.

The next morning the district was searched for clues and Police Constable George Ward found, in the field near where the lad Wilson had seen Peace go over the wall, an envelope addressed to "C. Peace Esq.". Nearby was a pile of notes and letters that were to throw a very different light upon the demure Mrs. Dyson, the devoted wife and mother, and her relationship with her husband's murderer.

The day after Dyson's death the enterprising reporters of the local newspapers interviewed Mrs. Dyson. To the representative of the *Sheffield Independent* she talked with great composure and forcefulness. She might be said to have shown eagerness to talk. Of Peace, she said: "He seemed at first to be a very kindly man, having birds and parrots and so on that he used to talk about. He enticed people to go in and talk. Mr. Dyson used to go in, but, after a while, Peace seemed to put an evil eye on us and he then threatened my life."

She recounted the incident when Peace had threatened her with a revolver in the presence of neighbours and added: "Peace has told people that Mr. Dyson owed him hundreds of pounds. He is a defamer and murderer." It is, of course, very likely that Peace did tell people this and it does raise the ugly suspicion that the Dysons were in agreement to fleece Peace as Mrs. Dyson led him on. But Peace's accusations against the Dysons covered a wide field. He often said that they were not married at all—a very serious social matter in Victorian times. In this point the Chief Constable of Sheffield was to make discreet inquiries, and he informed the Home Office that he had evidence of their proper matrimonial state.

Certainly readers of the Sheffield newspapers were informed, at length, by Mrs. Dyson that she, at any rate, in all this affair was one whose moral purity and social decorum were unassailable.

Two days later Mr. Dyson was buried. There were only four mourners, his widow, his little son, and his brothers, William and Henry. Even in death he was a lonely and somewhat pathetic figure. It is difficult not to feel sorrow for the refined, and perhaps rather priggish, Arthur Dyson. He had died bravely in defence of a woman who seems to have given him little peace and whose relationship with his murderer was, at best, ambiguous. He had borne gross insults and persecution in silence. He had attempted to fend off a cunning and malicious man by the futile gesture of throwing a message over a garden wall.

A shattered nervous system makes for timidity and social uncertainty, particularly in moments of violence or stress. Yet, when it came to the final decision of his life, he went unarmed to tackle his tormentor. Perhaps something of the pioneering Arthur Dyson, who had helped push the railroads across the American wilderness, was still there behind the bookish *façade* of an ailing man.

On December 8th there was an inquest at the Stagg Inn, Sharrow Head, Sheffield. It was to be the first public ordeal of Catherine Dyson. She described the early friendship with Peace and the course of events leading to Peace's hatred and persecution. On the night of the murder, she said, she had come out of the closet to find Peace, revolver in hand, in the yard. He had said: "Speak, or I fire," and she had screamed. Her husband had come to help her. Peace had walked off and her husband had made to follow. Peace had then shot him.

The Coroner, Mr. Wightman, said: "You are quite sure your husband never quarrelled with you on account of your familiarity with Peace?"

"No."

"You are quite sure?"

"Yes."

Her husband had told her not to talk to Peace so she had not done so.

Inspector Bradbury then handed the Coroner a packet of papers. Questioned by the Coroner, Mrs. Dyson denied flatly she had ever written to Peace. The Coroner said the packet handed to him appeared to be letters, but they were addressed to no one and might have been written by Mrs. Dyson, or might not. He read one: "I write to you these few lines to thank you for all your kindness."

Inspector Bradbury: "A constable found them next morning in a field near where Peace got over the wall. He (Peace) had been in the neighbourhood, to Mr. Newman's, and the 'Prince of Wales' and other places, showing these letters. He said Mrs. Dyson wrote them to him at different times when he lived at Darnall."

The Coroner said that some of the notes were in pencil and some in ink. One card, he said, was in Mr. Dyson's handwriting and requested Peace not to annoy his family. He asked Mrs. Dyson if she could identify the handwriting of the notes and letters. No, Mrs. Dyson could not. She had never written to Peace, she repeated.

The Coroner left it at that and, after some more formal evidence and a summing-up, the jury returned a verdict that Arthur Dyson had been wilfully murdered by Charles Peace. Commenting the next day on the inquest the *Sheffield Independent*, with, to modern readers, a staggering journalistic freedom, said: "All the letters indeed were such as would probably be written by a woman carrying on an intrigue, but inasmuch as Mrs. Dyson denied writing them, the Coroner was compelled to accept the answer and to hand them over to the care of the police."

There was no more to be done until Peace was arrested. The following description of him was widely circulated:—

"He is thin and slightly built, 46 years of age, but looks 10 years older. Five feet four or five inches in height, grey (nearly white) hair, beard and whiskers (the whiskers were long when he committed the murder, but may now be cut, or shaved off). Has lost one or more fingers off the left hand, cut marks on the back of each hand and one on forehead. Walks with legs rather wide apart, speaking somewhat peculiarly as though his tongue was too large for his mouth and is a great boaster. He is a joiner or picture frame maker, but occasionally cleans and repairs clocks and watches and sometimes deals in oleographs, engravings, pictures, etc. Associates with loose women and has been twice in penal servitude for burglaries near Manchester. Has lived in Manchester, Salford, Liverpool and Hull."

Later the police issued bills headed in large letters "MUR-

DER—ONE HUNDRED POUNDS REWARD", offering that sum for information leading to the discovery and conviction of Charles Peace.

But the months went by and there was no sign of Peace. To avoid what had now become unpleasant notoriety—and one suspects some hostility from her in-laws—Mrs. Dyson took her small son and returned to America to live with her sister in Cleveland.

It began to look as though Arthur Dyson would be unavenged.

CHAPTER FIVE

It was one of the strange complexities of his nature that Peace, like many criminals, could be lunatically impulsive in action and immediately afterwards cool and calculating in dealing with the flow of events from his own actions. After shooting down Arthur Dyson he fled into the darkness of the fields, and ran until the uproar of shouting voices faded behind him. He stopped and listened. No sounds. He stooped to see if he could see pursuers silhouetted against the skyline. There was no one after him. He slowed to a quick walk and began to plan what to do next.

During the period that lay ahead of him, he was to show one of the most extraordinary examples of criminal capacity in English history. It was to be the time when Peace, the long-term convict, the shabby man with the gun in his pocket, was to exhibit the full measure of his worth. He was to demonstrate his ability as a human fox, wits alerted to maximum cunning, not only keeping ahead of the pack of organised society behind him, but turning to loot that society on a grand scale.

He walked out of the fields into Endcliffe Woods. In the woods he stopped and put an india-rubber band over his head, confining his long whiskers under his chin. With his muffler drawn up tight it was a quick rough and ready disguise against a possible quick circularisation of a hunted man "with full whiskers". He then zig-zagged and doubled back through the Sheffield suburbs, on foot and by hailing cabs for short distances, until he had worked his way back into the centre of the city.

He went to Spring Street, where an aunt obligingly kept a cache of clothes and other props for him against just such emergencies as this. It was an elderly seafaring man with a short beard who emerged. It says much for the man's consummate impudence that he then calmly went to see his brother, Dan, whom he called out of a public house in Russell Steeet. He could not have known at that time how close the police were behind him. In fact, half-an-hour later the police, in their turn, called for Dan. Dan admitted he had seen Charlie, but registered great surprise and shock when told that he was now sought for murder.

Peace also called on his mother in Orchard Street and stayed with her for some time. They had quarrelled about Mrs. Dyson, but in times of serious trouble she always stood by "her Charlie" and, when the moment came for Charlie to slip quickly away into the night streets, they parted affectionately. It was to be the last time he saw her, though he made certain that by devious routes and messengers she always knew where he was and how he was faring.

He had now to get out of the city and he knew that the delays caused by family farewells had lengthened the odds against him. However, he walked boldly through the streets, ready to vanish into cover at the sight of a policeman. Peace's alertness was almost supernatural. Months later a Sheffield acquaintance, a respectable butcher, was in London on business when, walking over Holborn Viaduct, he saw approaching him, in morning coat and top hat, an undisguised Charlie Peace. Peace spotted him at the same moment and, the butcher afterwards told the police, in an instant he turned and dived down a flight of stairs towards the streets below. The butcher gave chase, but when he turned the first corner Peace had disappeared.

There were occasions during his life when detectives spotted him, but were unable to catch up with him because of his ability to mingle with a crowd and throw off pursuers by agility and speed in doubling about in city streets and courtyards. The night he shot Dyson he walked down from his mother's house to Attercliffe Railway Station. It has been said that police were already on duty watching for him there when he passed through, but never saw him. A late train was disgorging a party of racegoers. Many were drunk and unruly. In the confusion no-one saw the little sailor buy a ticket and catch a train to Rotherham. At Rotherham he left the train, walked to Mexborough Station and booked to Hull. At the intermediate station of Normanton he got off and caught a train to York. He stayed overnight in the Railway Hotel at York and the next morning caught a train to Beverley, where he handed in his ticket to Hull. He waited a while, then took a train to Cottingham and from there walked into Hull. It was just on ten o'clock when he walked in on his wife and family at their eating-house in Collier Street.

He was having his breakfast in the kitchen when two detectives entered the shop. Police Constable Pearson, of Sheffield Police, had travelled to Hull overnight to alert the police there and the first move was to question Mrs. Peace.

Peace ran quickly upstairs, climbed out of a bedroom window, scaled up a handy drainpipe and hid on the roof, while the two men searched the premises to the accompaniment of wails from Mrs. Peace that "not sight nor sound of Charlie had she seen these past weeks". When they had gone Peace got back into the house and stripped off his clothes for a wash. His wife and daughter stood sobbing in the room and there were high words about "that woman Dyson", whereupon Peace, in a fury, struck them both heavy blows. He was still stripped when policemen again walked into the shop. Once more Peace hid on the roof while the men stolidly tramped through the rooms, ignoring the women's denials of the presence of the master of the house.

The next day a woman living two hundred yards from the Peace house told the police that a man (whom she later identified by description as Peace) had jumped in through her garret window after making his way across the rooftops, threatened to hurt her if she screamed, waited until after nightfall and then slipped away into the street.

Detective Pearson, from Sheffield, later in the day called to see Mrs. Peace and found her with a rapidly blackening eye. She repeated that she had not seen her husband for weeks, was fed up with him and "his women" and the police might do what they liked with him. She did not mention that he had already obtained lodgings in another part of the town, in his favourite role of seaman, and was charming his landlady with a few gay airs on the violin.

The next day Peace himself spotted Pearson in the town, putting up "Wanted" notices containing his own full description. Noting the reference to his beard he decided the time had come to assume a full disguise.

He shaved off his beard completely, dyed his hair and assumed such a different personality that his step-son Willie passed him in the street without recognising him. Whereupon Peace, who had been hanging about to get a message to his wife, made himself known.

Peace stayed in Hull for three weeks "doing" some houses, then for some mysterious reason—perhaps he had been spotted by a detective, or thought informers were on his track, he decided to carry out a grand tour of burglary throughout most of England.

His first stop was at York where he went to the races. He found himself standing near to a Mr. Cooke, who had lived near him in Sheffield, but felt quite secure in his disguise and stayed where he was. There was a disturbance among a crowd of drunken militiamen and, during the ensuing riot, a mounted policeman nearly knocked Peace over. He made a great scene to a high-ranking police officer who was on duty, and received a handsome apology for the hasty behaviour of the man on horseback.

He was for a short time in Manchester. Mr. J. Henry, of Horsforth in Leeds, recounts the story that his mother, when a young unmarried woman, lived with her parents in Harpurley. The house next door was rented by a small, mysterious little man, who brought no furniture with him. He was always apologising for his lack of furniture. The man played the violin well and persuaded Mr. Henry's mother, who played the piano, to let him accompany her with his violin. She agreed, though in fact she disliked the new neighbour.

The little man vanished as mysteriously as he had come—and a little while later the family heard that the police were hunting Charles Peace. They also made another discovery. Their neighbour, whom Mr. Henry's mother firmly believed to be Peace—had knocked a small hole in the cellar wall and had been quietly taking coal from their cellar.

It may well have been that at this time Peace had decided to quit Manchester, for he told his family later that he had a bad scare when passing through a Manchester railway station—he saw a policeman he knew from Sheffield on duty there watching passers-by.

Though it is now nearly impossible to establish exactly all the places visited by Peace during the next few weeks it is known that he was in Doncaster, London, Bristol, Bath, Birmingham,

Oxford and Derby before making his way back to Hull. It seems to have been in the nature of a holiday after a period of hard exertion, for he said afterwards "I only 'worked' two or three houses a night to keep myself in money."

It was an agreeable way to see the countryside and there were the pleasures for a gregarious man of striking up brief travelling companionships and exchanging gossip and views without the difficulties of more persisting relationships. On a train between Bath and Oxford he found a congenial friend in a burly man who turned out to be a police sergeant making his way to Stafford Assizes. The sergeant was flattered when the little elderly man quizzed him about his interesting work. They chatted contentedly away until the train came to Didcot Junction. Both men had a four-hour wait for their connection and shared a supper and a few drinks (though the elderly man excused himself after the second glass), then slept side by side in the waiting-room at the station. On parting they shook hands, declared one another capital fellows and said what a pleasure it had been to meet. "Good luck," called out the sergeant, as his train pulled away, to the waving little figure on the platform.

On another journey Peace struck up a conversation with a somewhat taciturn middle-aged man with a look about him of one used to heavy responsibilities. At first he did not unbend, but Peace had a way with him and finally the man admitted, shyly but proudly, that he was Marwood, the famous executioner.

When the time came for Marwood to leave the train Peace shook his hand cordially and remarked: "If ever you have to do the job for me, be sure you grease the rope well to let me slip." Marwood went on his way laughing heartily at the suggestion that he would ever meet his benign acquaintance in the professional line.

There was one other occasion when Peace was in a train in what was more or less his own territory between Sheffield and Manchester. Perhaps informers had been at work, but certainly the police had a tip that Peace was on the train. Accordingly they stopped it at an intermediate station and began a search.

One of the detectives attempting to decide whether any of

the passengers looked suspicious was hampered in his efforts by the enthusiastic co-operation of a small elderly man with an ugly dark face, who insisted on helping him to find "that rascal". The old man hopped up and down the platform in great excitement, getting thoroughly in the way, offering obvious advice and little cries of encouragement.

The police drew a blank and the train was waved on again, the last man aboard being the elderly amateur detective, who jumped on to the moving train with great agility for one so patently decrepit, shouting to the somewhat embarrassed detectives: "Mind you keep a watch out now for that scamp—a sharp lookout, mind you."

The detectives would have been even more red-faced if they had realised that their willing helper was none other than Peace himself.

The detectives, of course, were not as foolish as they might appear to modern conceptions. They had no photographs to go on—for pictures were not widely circularised as they are now—only a general description. Not much help to find a man who could walk past members of his family so cunningly disguised that they did not recognise him.

It was at this time that Peace perfected one of his cleverest inventions. Hiding his injured hand was always a problem. He made a tube from a piece of fine gutta percha and put his injured hand and arm into this. There was a plate at the bottom of the tube and on this he fitted a small hook, which he used with great dexterity. The effect of a one-armed man was given the final touch of authenticity when at mealtimes he would replace the hook with a special fork arrangement. Indeed he was often congratulated, as well he might, by onlookers on his ingenuity in overcoming his "disability".

His real disability did help; the fact of a missing finger combined with a small hand enabled him to bend his thumb into the palm, making the whole fist small enough to fit comfortably—and without a suspicious thickness at the wrist—in the tube.

Early in the year 1877 Peace was in Nottingham. He had not been there before, but took a great liking to the place and its many opportunities for plunder. Acting on his principle that the closer a man is to the police the less likely he is to be suspected of wrongdoing, he took lodgings near the police station in Burton Road.

He did a certain amount of "work" in the city and by loafing about low public-houses struck up some acquaintances among the city's thieves. In this way he was put in touch with a Mrs. Adamson, who was a notorious "fence", or receiver of stolen property, in the district. Soon afterwards he went to lodge with her in her house in the Marsh area. It was in this house that he was to meet a woman whose effect on his life was to be as important as Mrs. Dyson's.

One evening he was having his tea at the house when a young woman entered the room. Peace, always susceptible to feminine charms, was immediately all attention. The woman was something of the same type in appearance (though, as he was to discover, not in character) as Mrs. Dyson. She was tall, well-proportioned, if rather stout for modern taste, with a profusion of brown hair and dark, bold eyes. The bold eyes went well with a somewhat provocative manner. This was Mrs. Susan (usually known as Sue) Bailey, now also resident with Mrs. Adamson after somewhat absentmindedly mislaying her husband.

Born Susan Gray in 1842, of a family of small business folk in Nottingham, she was designed by nature to drift into just such a house as that of Mrs. Adamson's and eventually into the life of someone like Charles Peace. In her childhood she had a sweet voice and was eagerly sought for various church choirs. This was one of her strongest attractions for Peace—her knowledge of church music and ability to sing hymns in a clear soprano voice.

Her early life had been uneventful. She had helped her father by keeping his books. She had then drifted into keeping books for a commercial traveller called Bailey who came to call on her father. She said herself: "One day he asked me to marry him. In a spirit of vexation, I, having had some little disturbance with a brother of mine, said 'yes' ".

The marriage was not a success and she left her husband only three weeks after the ceremony. It is perhaps typical of her character that one day on her way to chapel she met Bailey in the street, he asked her to return and she agreed as casually as she had left him. They stuck it out for a year, then split up again. When she met Peace, Bailey was giving her a small allowance, but she claimed her main income came from sewing lace caps for women. It is possible, but it seems odd that a respectable married woman, even if separated from her husband, should be living in a house with someone like Mrs. Adamson.

She was not at first attracted to "the one-armed man", whose appearance she considered to be rather odd. However, she sat down at the tea table and lowered her eyes demurely as her fellow lodger gazed at her steadily, a somewhat terrifying expression of infatuation on his face. Peace asked Mrs. Adamson if the newcomer was her daughter. For some purpose of her own, perhaps to restrain Peace's obviously amorous intentions, Mrs. Adamson said she was.

Peace started to mutter to Mrs. Adamson, who told him: "You can speak before her. She won't say anything," a remark that illuminates Mrs. Bailey's reputation. Peace and Mrs. Adamson then spoke openly about a business deal, Peace had "acquired" some cigars and wished Mrs. Adamson to sell them for him. She did so, obtaining 18s. of which she got 6s. commission.

From then on, whenever Mrs. Bailey was at breakfast, dinner, tea or supper, her new acquaintance seemed to be there at the same time. He insisted that he was a hawker, but did not pursue this fiction long, openly fetching into the house silverware and other stolen property.

Some two years later Sue was to give a reporter on the *Sheffield Independent* a vivid, if somewhat garbled account of her strange wooing by Peace.

"On one occasion he went out of town, saying he had to go and see his mother at Hull. By his mother he meant Hannah Peace. Peace on that occasion took £5 to Mrs. Ward at Hull and stayed there three weeks. During that time he committed several robberies either in Hull or the neighbourhood . . . he told me that on one occasion he had to run for it when he 'fired wide' at a policeman by whom he was in imminent danger of capture.

"He returned after a while to Nottingham. I was out at the time of his return, having business in the evening, for I was still at work and getting my own living in an honest way. I was not earning much for work was short, but still it was honest.

"On this particular night on my return home Mrs. Adamson said to me, 'Oh, Mrs. Bailey, who do you think has come back?' I replied that I did not know to which she made answer, 'Why, the one-armed old man and he has asked for you. He swears he will shoot you unless you go to him'."

Peace had in fact taken lodgings in the house next door, and the woman who owned the house then came in to say: "Oh Mrs. Bailey, do come in, the old man's gone mad, he wants to see you so bad. He won't be satisfied with anyone until you go."

Sue agreed to go and see the "old man", whom she found drunk. "Is that you pet?" he called out and on being assured it was, asked if she was not pleased to see him. Sue said she was, made him a cup of tea and stayed with him until he seemed restored to an even keel.

"The following day he came very early and he said he was sorry he had been in such a bad way and had behaved so rudely. He next asked me to stay at home that day. I said, 'No, that would not do. I should lose my work.' 'Never mind that,' he said. He reckoned up how much I was earning and said, 'Look here, darling, if you will promise me not to go to work again, I will pay your board and lodgings. And if Mrs. Adamson likes I will give her 14s. a week for my board and come and stay, but not sleep here'."

Despite the somewhat unconventional courtship Sue added "Eventually my better feelings were overruled and I submitted myself to him. He was invariably very kind to me and I did not live with him unhappily."

Shortly afterwards the couple moved to another lodging-house as Mr. and Mrs. Thompson and set up house together. Now that his expenses were increased Peace embarked on an orgy of burglary. He hired a shop in a quiet street and gave it out that he was a manufacturer of marking ink. From this hide-out for his tools and stolen goods, he travelled far and wide to "work". In June he was seen entering a house in Nottingham, but drew his pistol and ran. He dashed through a nearby stable, over a wall and through a wood yard. There was a man working in the yard who made as though to bar the fugitive's way. Peace pointed his revolver and told him to stand aside or pay the consequences. Sullenly the man drew back and Peace escaped into the streets nearby.

He was now so bold that he returned to Sheffield, making his way back into the city quite openly. Peace claimed that he saw Inspector Bradbury, the man in charge of the case of the Banner Cross murder, and actually walked past him without the policeman recognising him. That night he broke into a house in Havelock Square and got away with a rich haul of jewellery. He was still in the house when by accident he made a noise. Through a window he saw a passing watchman stop and look up at the house. At the same time a police sergeant came up and the two men started talking together, looking towards the house. Peace fled through a rear window.

Back in Nottingham again with his beloved Sue, Peace robbed, in quick succession, a big tailors' establishment and a number of private houses. Then he went on to break into a factory in Derby, a nobleman's house at Melton Mowbray, from which he took several hundreds of pounds' worth of jewels and silver plate in perhaps the best single haul of his career, and a furrier's in Worksop.

He felt he had earned a holiday and wished, sentimentally, to show Sue some of his old haunts. They moved to Hull and became the star boarders occupying two front rooms in the home of a police sergeant in Aubury Road. They were to stay there for two months, the sergeant and Peace getting into the way of having long chats together in the front parlour, while "Mrs. Thompson" hovered solicitously with refreshments. It has been said that at least once Peace drew his landlord's attention to burglaries he had committed himself and listened gravely as the man gave his professional verdict on the raids.

At first, however, Peace was idle, enjoying his break from "work". He escorted Sue round to see the sights, the ships in from foreign countries and the fishing trawlers landing their catches; to pleasant evenings at "smokers" at the more respectable public houses and on excursions to neighbouring places of interest.

They took a stroll one day down Collier Street and Peace saw that Hannah was still in business. On some pretext he persuaded Sue to take a message to her. On instructions Sue merely handed the message to Hannah, and left without giving her time to ask questions. Mrs. Peace read the note: "I am waiting to see you just up Anlaby Road". She called Willie and together they made their way to the rendezvous.

As they walked up Anlaby Road they were astonished to see their missing husband and step-father waiting quite openly to greet them. He was smartly dressed in black coat and trousers, black velvet waistcoat and tall hat. A pair of expensive kid gloves were on his hands, he was twirling a cane and a well-trained little fox terrier frisked at his heels. There was a joyful reunion and Peace and his family strolled about the streets for a while. Peace told them where he was staying—but did not mention "Mrs. Thompson"—and on parting said he would send for them when he was able to do so. Refreshed by family good wishes and expressions of affection Peace then returned to tea at the genial police sergeant's parlour.

It had been a splendid holiday, but now funds were running short again. Back to "work". There were too many fine opportunities to be missed in Hull, so the police soon found themselves plagued by an epidemic of night raids on the gentlemen's houses in the town. One particular incident told them only too clearly that they were dealing with a desperate, as well as a resourceful man.

Peace had been watching a house in Lister Street and one Saturday evening about nine o'clock, when all seemed dark and quiet, he got in and began to collect together everything he could find of value. He was still ransacking the house when he heard the key turn in the front door. Moving quickly to the landing on the first floor he looked over the banisters and saw two women and two men taking off their coats and wraps in the hall below.

He was creeping away to make his way out through the back, when he heard the sound of the party climbing the staircase. He jumped back towards the banisters, pointed his revolver over it and fired a bullet into the ceiling of the hall. The two women screamed, the men cursed and the party ran back down the stairs. Peace was able to fling up a rear window, let himself down to full length on his arms by hanging on to the windowsill, and dropped into the garden below. He ran across the garden and over the wall into the roadway. One of the men in the house had plucked up courage to run round from the front of the house in pursuit. Still running Peace pointed his revolver over his shoulder and fired. A few paces further on he looked back and saw the man had fled back into cover.

Another night Peace was prowling about near some likely houses when he saw the policeman on patrol was drunk. Seizing his chance he broke into six houses in a row and came away with his pockets stuffed with silver spoons, knives and forks and plates. The policeman was subsequently dismissed from the Force.

Another policeman was more alert. He spotted Peace coming out of a house and stopped him in the road. "What are you doing there?" he wanted to know. Peace stepped quickly back, drew his revolver and said: "What's it to you?" firing as he did so. The policeman, sensibly, made only a token attempt to stop the fugitive from running away into the dark. He could have done nothing against an armed man, though Peace claimed "I fired wide on purpose".

From time to time, when he had accumulated enough stolen property in his lodgings, Peace would make a trip away to dispose of the valuables, telling his police sergeant landlord that he was a dealer, buying and selling goods. Just where and to whom the goods went was never known.

Peace's impudence was growing with his apparent impunity from arrest. Reading that one of the town councillors was to give a dinner party, Peace broke into the man's house the night before and found all the gold and silver plate laid out ready for use. He swept it up into a sack, sneaked out of the house and hid the swag in an empty house nearby, calling for it later when the coast seemed clear.

It is an unverifiable story, but a likely one, that while in Hull Peace used empty houses to store his growing pile of goods, in one case using a house where he knew the occupants were away. It is said that he entered and left the house quite openly by the front door, which he opened with a skeleton key, dressed in the clothes of a clergyman.

But with the instinct of a wild animal Peace sensed that the time had come to leave Hull. He had roused the police to a fury that meant they would move heaven and earth to catch him. He told his policeman landlord that business forced him to move to London. There was a pleasant farewell evening of song and music—provided by the talented Mr. and Mrs. Thompson—

then back to Nottingham and Mrs. Adamson's lodgings.

Business was indeed brisk. Peace "worked" Nottingham with great industry and, in company with companions recruited from the local underworld, raided a silkware house in the Market Place for over £300 worth of goods. Perhaps the linking up with the local criminals was a mistake, for as always in that world informers began to whisper along the grapevine. There was talk of a "new 'un" with Mrs. Adamson. The talk reached the ears of detectives. The word went out to take a look at this man.

Mr. and Mrs. Thompson were respectably in bed at Mrs. Adamson's, one evening about ten o'clock, when a police inspector came into the room without ceremony. Sue was asleep, but Peace was quickly on the alert. "Hullo," he said to the policeman, "what do you want?"

"What's your name?" The inspector was not wasting time with civilities.

"John Ward."

"Where do you come from?"

"Tunbridge Wells."

"What trade are you?"

"What's that to you?"

"I want a civil answer."

"I'm a hawker."

"Where's your stock?"

Peace said that it was downstairs and if the inspector cared to go down and wait he and his wife would dress and come and show it to him. Amazingly enough the inspector agreed and left the room, "as soft as a barm," as Peace said later.

As soon as he had gone Peace was out of bed and huddling into his clothes. "See you in the morning," he told the awake, and now thoroughly alarmed Sue. "Don't worry, they've nought against you." The window of the room was barred by steel rods only a few inches apart, but somehow Peace managed to squeeze his way through, dropping lightly in his stockinged feet into the yard below. He dropped almost in front of a man, a neighbour of Mrs. Adamson, standing in the yard. "The 'Bobbies' are after me for neglecting my wife and family," Peace told him. Sympathetically the man agreed to keep quiet. Leaving the yard by a passageway past a public-house Peace was spotted by the landlady of the 'pub', who was startled to see a man walking in the middle of the night without boots. To her Peace told the same tale and she agreed not to give the alarm.

He took refuge in the house of a friend of Mrs. Adamson's, not forty yards from the house from which he had fled. He calmly sent her back to the house to collect his boots, telling her: "Mind now the 'Bobbies' don't see you." He walked through the night to a lodging house several miles away and the next morning gave a child a shilling to take a note of his whereabouts to Sue. She joined him there and told him that the police inspector had been furiously angry when he had discovered 'John Ward' had gone, but had been unable to find any excuse to arrest her. In those days policemen were not surprised to meet with sullen silence and lack of assistance in such rough districts.

The couple stayed in hiding in various lodging-houses in Nottingham for a few days, then Peace decided the time had come to do what many ambitious provincials feel they should do—try his luck in London. Accordingly they moved to London and took up residence at 25, Stangate Street, Lambeth. Peace proceeded to break into four or five houses a night for a period of a fortnight.

He broke into Lord Shaftesbury's large town house at Wandsworth and stole several hundred pounds' worth of jewels and plate. The house was such a rich repository of treasure that Peace decided it was worth a second visit. Six weeks later he paid a second visit to his Lordship's home and, as he put it himself "brought away what I was unable to carry off the first time".

From this time on, and for the next eighteen months, Peace was out night after night burgling houses not only in London, but throughout southern England, often several houses a night. He could enter and ransack a house, even one full of sleeping occupants, within a few minutes, though if worried by the presence of a policeman outside, or by movement within the house, he would wait motionless and silent for as long as an hour, before leaving the premises.

There was soon plenty of cash in hand and Peace and Sue moved from their one room lodging in Lambeth to a small house in Crane Court, Greenwich. There, they were joined by Hannah and Willie. The reasons for this are not clear. One story is that Sue discovered for the first time that her unlawful spouse was Charles Peace, the Banner Cross murderer. Some reports have it that she found an In Memoriam card to Peace's little boy who had died in infancy; others that he was foolish enough to boast to her one day that "They would give £100 for me at Darnall", she subsequently wheedled out of him the true story and from this moment on he was never too certain of her and needed the faithful Hannah to act as a watchdog.

Another version is that Peace had heard that Hannah's business in Hull was not prospering and it was not safe to have her away from his control in case she too was tempted by the £100 reward. This story has it that Sue and Peace went to Hull and persuaded Mrs. Peace to come south in the expectation of being set up in business in Tottenham Court Road.

The truth is probably more simple. Peace always kept in touch with Hannah and she, knowing that he was doing well in London, probably felt that as the lawful wife she was entitled to share some of the luxury. Whatever the motivation, later that year Hannah and Willie were in London, living in a house next door to that occupied by Peace and Sue in Billingsgate Street, Greenwich. Peace rented both houses for his dependents and all seems to have been harmony for a time. Unfortunately this happy state of affairs was not to persist when Sue and Hannah were actually living in the same house.

There seems little doubt that it was not until this period that Sue knew that Thompson was Peace. It is one thing to live with a burglar, quite another to live with a murderer, and her manner towards him changed in a way that Peace was far too clever to miss. He never wholly trusted Sue after this—indeed trusting a woman of Sue's nature in any circumstances would be folly—and began to watch her closely. She was not encouraged to go out without him. She had always been fond, too fond, of drink and under the strain of being watched she began to drink heavily. Despite these domestic problems Peace was still very much master of his fate. He felt he had now reached that time of life when he owed it to himself to move into better surroundings. He was now in his middle forties, though contriving for disguise and other reasons to look much older. He had shaved the hair at the front and used walnut juice to stain his face and head to a rich brown hue.

He proceeded to go house hunting. His needs were specific. The house must be large, in a respectable area and handy for those districts where "work" was promising. It took a little time to find one quite suitable, but finally he heard that there was a most pleasant villa for lease at 5, East Terrace, Evelina Road, Peckham. When he saw it and inspected the premises he realised that it was almost perfect. Its site was particularly ideal, just by a railway embankment, which made the task of entering and leaving the house at night without being seen much easier, and also handy for the districts of Blackheath, Greenwich, and other South London areas full of gentlemen's houses. It had eight rooms and a large garden and a front and rear exit—just in case the householder might be disturbed by people he did not wish to see. It was not cheap, of course, the rental being £30 a year.

There was a slight snag when he sought out the owner, Mr. Samuel Smith, a builder's foreman, of Peckham, who was doing a little speculating in property on his own account. Mr. Smith would like references, please. "Certainly," said Peace, "come and have dinner with me at my home in Greenwich and you shall have them." Mr. Smith went to dinner at Billingsgate Street, where he could see that Mr. Thompson was a man of substance. He was dined well, Mr. Thompson paid a quarter's rent in advance and somehow the question of references was quite overlooked—absurd to suspect such an affable old man as Mr. Thompson.

The residents in Evelina Road were interested to see the new family arrive and to watch the large quantities of expensive furniture and the appurtenances of respectable well-to-do middle class living being off-loaded from carriers' carts and borne into 5, East Terrace. They noted with satisfaction that Mr. and Mrs. Thompson were well dressed. The district's tone was being maintained.

Peace was determined to live in the cosy domestic way some part of his strange soul yearned for. To do it he was to keep up for months, in the face of mounting hazards, the dual, if not triple roles of church-going householder and local worthy, production-line robber of houses and controller of two mutually antagonistic women who could have given him away at any time in a moment of feminine pique.

He had always been fond of gardening; now he took it up in a big way, planting rows of expensive flowers in the garden behind the house. He built up a collection of pets, including ten guinea pigs, a goat, two cats, two dogs, a cockatoo, a parrot and four pigeons, all of which he fed daily on a balanced diet worked out by himself. He went regularly to St. Antholin's Church nearby—it was known for the excellence of its church music—and ingratiated himself with his neighbours as the soul of kindness and propriety.

Very soon after he had moved in he set to to build himself a small stable in the garden, and into this was introduced a smart pony, called Tommy, and a handy little gig.

During one of his night expeditions Peace had visited Southampton and got into an office in Above Bar. He had found there a large safe that defied even his skill. He looked through the office papers, discovered the address of the owner of the office, went to the house, broke in, walked up to the main bedroom and made a search, found the office keys in the pocket of some trousers hung over a chair, and walked out again. He returned to the office, opened the safe and took out some £200 cash. In his new role of established citizen he felt he should invest this money, so he bought Tommy and the gig to enable him to travel further afield on "business".

While building the stables he also took the opportunity to knock up a wooden fence right round the garden, which he said screened his plants from the wind. It also had the other purpose of effectively screening the garden and back of the house from view, but chosen neighbours were invited in to see Tommy, whom his master had trained to do several tricks.

One of these was to lie down and "die" and remain absolutely still at a word of command. Another skill Tommy had learned was to walk at slow march. Remarked one admiring onlooker: "Why I declare you cannot hear that animal's hoofs on the flags, so stately does he walk." Indeed, on night expeditions, this was true—Peace had seen to that.

Mr. Thompson was rarely seen in the mornings. He was delicate, it seemed, and must lie abed. His nights were restless—as a growing number of householders and infuriated policemen could testify. He was "working" by two main methods. There were the early evening "jobs", when he was accustomed to scale the porticos, or climb up the drainpipes, and loot the top rooms while the family and servants were busy with dinner below, or the raids in the early hours of the mornings, when he could loot houses at leisure. Willie would wait with the faithful Tommy and gig nearby, ready to whisk him away home through the dawn streets.

Back home there would be the pleasure of sitting enjoying the ministrations of a fond Sue, to whom his greeting was invariably "Well, Pet, have you not got a smile for me?" This would call for a tender kiss and then, according to whether the night had been successful or not: "I have not done much, my girl," or "I have done pretty well." He would spend some moments examining the proceeds, then go to bed until midday.

The appointments at 5, East Terrace, grew steadily more opulent. There was the walnut furniture, the bijou piano, the beaded slippers and a vast collection of musical instruments—so many, in fact, that Mr. Thompson had to ask a neighbour to rent him a room to store them. There were many musical evenings, when a chosen selection of local friends would be asked to join them. Mr. Smith, the house's owner, was a regular visitor. He was more than ever pleased with himself in his good sense in choosing Mr. and Mrs. Thompson as tenants. The hospitality was lavish and served on the best gold and silver plate.

It was a little puzzling that Mrs. Thompson herself did all the waiting on guests. It seemed strange that a family so comfortably placed did not keep the usual servant girl—a standard feature of even the humblest middle class homes—but Mr. Thompson said he did not hold with servants. They were always gossiping, which he held to be a fault he could not condone.

The ladies of the district had not missed the fact that Mrs. Thompson was always superbly gowned in a variety of expensive creations. She made a number of local friends, though Mr. Thompson did not care for her going out without him. He himself was fond of getting out and about—sometimes out of sheer good nature he would use Tommy and the gig to drive an acquaintance, who collected rents in Dulwich, around his area. Quite naturally he would discuss with his friend who lived in which house; did they seem people of consequence, judging by their way of life; or, "Was that a dog I heard barking as you went up the drive?"

There were the jaunts to Bow Street to watch the procession of human wreckage through the dock—a great moral lesson to a philosopher and student of his fellow men. None of his acquaintances who knew of his great interest in crime were surprised to learn, when a number of detectives from Great Scotland Yard were charged with conspiracy in connection with bribes, that Mr. Thompson intended to attend the trial.

There was one snag. The case was a *cause célèbre* and tickets for the court hearing were being allocated by a high ranking officer at Scotland Yard in person. It was necessary to attend there to make application. Mr. Thompson, respectable in black coat, top hat and gold spectacles, made his way there to ask for two tickets. He took with him a companion—it may well have been Willie, though this is not certain—who knew Mr. Thompson's real identity.

At Great Scotland Yard Mr. Thompson was ushered into a Superintendent's office, where he made his application for the tickets. He had brought with him a number of references from friends in Peckham. While these and the application were being considered Mr. Thompson and his friend were asked to wait without in the General Office.

Thoroughly at home Mr. Thompson strolled about the room, reading the various notices posted upon the walls. One of them offered £100 reward for the capture of Charles Peace in connection with the Banner Cross murder. Mr. Thompson pointed at this with his stick: "Have they caught that scamp, I wonder?"

His companion could only murmur somewhat uneasily: "I don't remember." No doubt he was relieved when Mr. Thompson was summoned to be told that he might have tickets for part of the trial of the detectives. Peace walked calmly out into the streets again, where he assured his sweating companion that he could "duff (bluff) all the bobbies in London."

At Whitsuntide Jane Anne Peace, who had recently married her childhood sweetheart William Bolsover, was invited to spend a few days with her husband at Evelina Road. They spent over a week there, being shown the sights of London by the bride's father, who paternally saw to it that they had enough spending money to make the visit enjoyable.

Peace was immersed in a project that he felt might well earn him a legitimate fortune. He had made the acquaintance of Mr. Henry Forsey Brion, of nearby Philips Road, Peckham. Mr. Brion seems to have been one of those characters who were legion in Victorian times. Moderately well-to-do, he was able to cultivate his character as an eccentric. In his case it took the form of imagining himself a great inventor. He had, for example, exhibited at the Mansion House in the City a map of a scheme he had drawn up to render the Sahara Desert fertile. The idea was to build a large canal from the Atlantic Ocean across a large tract of Africa and let in water to flood the great inland waste. He was delighted to find in Mr. Thompson a crony of like ingenuity of mind.

The two men concocted a scheme for raising sunken ships by pumping air into the hulls. At first it seems likely Peace was interested in the idea as a cover for certain rather more nefarious hobbies, such as the melting down of silver and gold plate and breaking up recognizable jewellery. He kept his own melting pot for dealing with the plate. Now, in his role of inventor, he could openly rig up a workshop.

However as time went by he seems to have become genuinely enthusiastic. Mr. Brion was at East Terrace morning and afternoon for days on end. They tackled other problems—the creation of a helmet to enable firemen to enter smoke-filled buildings was one—but they considered their greatest chance of success was with the ship-raising invention. Scale models were tried out at a local pond and, when they felt the time was ripe, they applied for a patent and set out to market their idea. They approached the Admiralty and the German Navy, but without success. Full of enthusiasm, they visited the Houses of Parliament together and tried to buttonhole M.P.s, but could not obtain backing.

Undaunted by their initial setback the two inventors worked on, Mr. Brion advancing quite a sum of money to further the good cause. Unhappily it is always difficult for creative minds to work together in harness. One day Mr. Brion took away a piece of equipment from East Terrace with the intention of showing it to another man, who they hoped would put up a further £500 towards the scheme's development.

Perhaps in this innocent move Peace saw just such a piece of trickery as he might have contemplated himself. He flew into a terrible rage, raced round to Mr. Brion's home and there was a furious scene. Eventually Peace left, muttering threats, and Mr. Brion congratulated himself that he had shown just the right amount of firmness in dealing with an awkward customer. When informed later of his friend's true character it is likely he had some retrospective nightmares—as well he might, for Peace returned to East Terrace and told Sue that if Brion appeared there again he would shoot him.

It may be that Peace was irritable in the way that night workers often are after a period of particularly hard work. The number of burglaries in south London had now reached such alarming proportions that the police were especially alert and extra night patrols were organised. Still the raids went on and the elusive prowler continued to defy all efforts to catch him.

Night after night Peace was out "working" and he had some narrow shaves before getting safely home to his own fireside. He was out one evening and climbed into a house when the family were at dinner. Peace was ransacking an upstairs room when a servant came in. The servant turned and ran downstairs and Peace scrambled through the window on to the roof of an outhouse and down into the yard at the rear of the house. The owner of the house loosed a dog which sprang furiously at Peace, who drew his pistol and shot the animal dead before making off.

On another night in the early hours two patrolling policemen saw a suspicious light in an upstairs window. They asked to be allowed to search the house and from an attic window one of the policemen saw Peace crouched on the roof. Courageously he started out of the window after him. Peace scuttled over the roof to a drainpipe, but in doing so cut his foot severely, for he had left his boots in the attic to save making a noise on the roof. Despite the deep cut and a steady flow of blood he managed to slide down the pipe and make his escape.

He had hardly recovered from this hurt when he fell while burgling a house in the centre of London and dropped on to the spiked railings surrounding the basement area which were so common a feature of houses of the period. By sheer good luck he escaped serious internal injury and was able to climb off the railings and get away.

As befitted a man who had once earned his living as an acrobat Peace's agility was that of a human monkey. Though he usually worked on his own he must have had contacts with London criminals, for one night an informer tipped off the detectives that a well-known burglar was going to enter a house in Westbourne Park. He did not know which one, so the detectives adopted the strategy of surrounding the area and putting a piece of black silk all along the railings before the houses so that any intruder would have to break it to get it. Peace got into one of the houses and was quietly at work, when the police patrol saw where he had broken the thread. They waited outside and as Peace climbed out of a window they made a dash up the garden to catch him. Peace turned and ran round the house, down the garden and leapt for some wooden trelliswork on a wall dividing the garden from the roadway. He swung up over the top of the wall, dropped into the road and was out of sight by the time the police had scrambled up behind him. The police were only able to find consolation for his escape in that he had dropped in the garden a carpetbag full of valuables.

With such a wave of burglaries it was not surprising that one of Mr. Thompson's friends at Peckham, knowing the inventor's skill with things mechanical, should ask him to inspect his own home with a view to suggesting anti-burglar devices. Mr. Thompson made a thorough job of examining the premises, suggesting a bolt here, a window catch there and the advantages of a padlock just here. Unhappily for the householder he was burgled a few nights later by a thief who seemed to have found the one way in that Mr. Thompson had overlooked. "A clever fellow, that," was Mr. Thompson's grave comment.

It would have taken a veritable fortress to bar the way to Peace. He had spotted one large house near Denmark Hill. Choosing his night he scaled a drainpipe up to a handy bedroom window. Here he found that an ingenious device prevented him, even after he had forced the catch, from opening the window more than two inches. He withdrew for that night but was determined to get in somehow. A few nights later he came back with an augmented supply of tools. He then proceeded to remove the whole window frame—in the way that house removers do to effect the entry of large pieces of furniture—got in and stole a valuable collection of jewellery.

He had accumulated a large quantity of tools, which he sometimes carried to the scene of operations in a violin case, sometimes in the gig. He devised a folding stepladder of pieces of wood which could be made to stretch upwards and be hooked onto a windowsill, but he did not use it often. He preferred a handy drainpipe for reaching upstairs windows. He also created some home-made candle lanterns from matchboxes and a cigar case. Folding shutters kept the light down to a minimum and were designed for the extinction of the candle with one quick movement of the hand.

Though Peace always insisted that he worked alone, there is strong evidence that from time to time he did associate with other thieves. The famous advocate, Sir Edward Marshall Hall, was sure that on one occasion by quickwittedness he had forced Peace and a gang of associates to abandon a burgling foray. The story is told in his life story by Mr. Marjoribanks.

When he was a boy Sir Edward was a keen collector of firearms. One day at his home in Horsham he was practising with a pistol, when three men came into the garden and said they were selling plaster statuettes. One member of the party was an undersized, emaciated man who said he was going up to the house "to get a drink of water".

Sir Edward saw that the men were taking stock of the house and garden so he bought one of the statuettes, put it up on a wall and shot it to pieces with a display of skilled marksmanship. One of the men asked him "Why do that?". Fixing him with a steady eye and still dangling his pistol in his hand Marshall Hall replied: "Because there are burglars about". The men left somewhat hurriedly, but that same night a neighbour's house was entered.

Some time later Marshall Hall saw Peace in the dock and recognized him as the little man who had asked for the drink of water.

One tragedy marred this happy period for Peace and depressed him for days. His faithful pony, Tommy, contracted a chill during one night expedition and despite devoted nursing by Peace, who sat up with him for several nights, died. Peace wept for hours, sitting huddled on a stool by the body. It was a business as well as a sentimental loss, but there was a ready solution to hand. Shortly afterwards Peace accosted a local milkman, explained sadly that his stable was now empty and he would gladly accommodate the milkman's horse rent-free. Glad to save money, the milkman agreed and the horse was moved into East Terrace. The milkman, however, was surprised that from this time on his normally strong and willing beast became a bad worker. Fortunately for Peace the animal could not tell his master that often he had done a night's work before starting on his milk round.

It was the sort of situation that had a strong appeal for Peace's always ready sense of humour. One day he had called into a chemist's shop near his home smoking an excellent cigar. The chemist remarked that it was a good cigar and asked: "Where did you get it?"

Peace replied, quite truthfully: "I stole it".

Chuckling at the waggishness of the churchgoing "Mr. Thompson", the chemist countered: "Wish you would steal one for me."

"I shall be only too happy."

Some while later "Mr. Thompson" again appeared in the shop and put a number of cigars on the counter. "You see I have not forgotten my promise. I have stolen these for you."

Late one night he was in the stables sorting out some property he had just stolen when a local constable, hearing a noise, came to see that everything was all right. Hearing his footsteps Peace threw the goods into a box and slammed down the lid. "Oh, come in, officer," he called out cheerfully as the constable appeared in the doorway, "I was just working on my invention. It would never do to let anyone see into this—" slapping the box with his hand as he did so. Satisfied the policeman bade him good night and left.

Despite his unfailing nerve, as the autumn of 1878 drew on Peace was hard pressed to keep up his facade. He was having some difficulty controlling his household. Sue was finding it a great strain to live with a man she now knew to be a murderer on the run, with the silent contemptous wife and the hostile stepson, both of whom treated her with a derisive stony indifference.

In hard times Sue had one panacea—the gin bottle. She now proceeded to tipple day and night. Even Peace, who never entirely lost his affection for her, later remarked bitterly: "She was a dreadful woman for drink and snuff. She snuffed half an ounce a day. As for drink I have paid as much as £3 in two days for her"—a large sum in the days when gin cost a few shillings a bottle.

The atmosphere at 5, East Terrace grew into one of jealousy, suspicion and fear. Peace could never be wholly free of the dread that the babblings of a drunken woman might give him away. Sue herself went in increasing terror of him. She said later: "I was not allowed to move from the house without either one or other of them being with me. I have been threatened and latterly at times he ill-treated me. I have had a pistol pointed at my head and more than once he threatened to kill me. He used occasionally to ill-use Hannah cruelly and in a way I shudder to think about.

"On one occasion he threatened me because I had pawned a silk dress (for drink) and he was afraid it might be traced. Racked by jealousy, a prey to remorse and the object of constant suspicion is it to be wondered at that I took to drinking? In this respect Peace was indulgent for though he jealously guarded me when I went out, at home I could have what I liked, and with drink deadened my senses and fled from my shame and despair."

Peace went on "working" night after night. One night he entered a large London mansion and saw in the main bedroom that the sleeping wife had a gold watch and chain under her pillow. He shifted her slightly and took the watch. The woman, thinking it was her husband who had touched her, muttered a fond word.

Peace crept home through the streets, not now to an affectionate greeting, but only the ramblings of a fuddled creature whose rosy good looks were rapidly deteriorating into a gaunt mask. Neighbours began to wonder what had happened to the once attractive woman.

Loyally Hannah played her part. She told them: "Mrs. Thompson's drinking is worrying Mr. Thompson a great deal. He's such a temperate man hisself, he cannot abide drunken folk. Not that he's not good to her. He does not care what she costs him in dress. He has never refused her anything. She could swim in gold if she wished, if only she would keep off the drink."

Sue had made friends with a Mrs. Long, who lived nearby in Kimberley Road, Peckham. Indeed she was in the habit of borrowing small sums of money from her—no doubt "to wet her whistle"—though Peace had forbidden her to do so. He was determined to arouse no suspicion of his financial status in the district, paying tradesmen with cash for any purchases. One day, when Peace was out, Sue managed to elude Hannah and fled to see Mrs. Long. That morning during an argument Peace had struck her a violent blow, and her face was badly cut. Comforted by Mrs. Long, Sue began to pour out a long rather disjointed account about how she had left home to live with Mr. Thompson, who was of independent means and who liked to travel about. She insisted that she was properly married to "the old villain"—a very doubtful claim, though bigamy would hardly have worried Peace—but that even at the church she knew she had made a mistake. She then burst into tears and spoke of the respectability of her relatives in the North and how she wished she had never left them.

It was a hair's-breadth escape for Peace, for there is little doubt that with some prompting she would have told the whole tale. However, at that moment she looked through the window and saw Peace, with Hannah beside him, driving past in a cab, no doubt in search of her. Some whim of feminine jealousy changed her mind. "No I'll not leave him. He would like me to leave, but I will assert my rights as a wife."

Back she went to East Terrace to a redoubled vigilance on the part of Peace and Hannah. Whenever Sue appeared at a neighbour's house, Hannah would be close behind. One day Sue did seize an opportunity to say to Mrs. Long: "Oh, Mrs. Long, if only I could tell you something—," then broke off abruptly.

Mr. Long, a milkman, had until that time been delivering supplies to 5, East Terrace. The day after this incident he received a message from Thompson that he was not to call again. A few days later the Longs were walking in the street when they saw a distraught Sue coming towards them. She hurried past without a word, and close behind her came

Mr. Thompson carrying a driving whip. He paused to wish the Longs a civil "Good morning" before pressing on after Sue.

Just how the situation would have resolved itself it is difficult to know, but at long last Peace's luck was to run out. There was the evening of October 10th, with its pleasant musical evening so reminiscent of happier times, when Peace set out on the expedition that was to bring him across the path of Police Constable Robinson in the Blackheath garden.

When he did not return the household was not at first too alarmed, but later in the day there was a knock on the door and a furtive messenger slipped a note into Hannah's hand. They knew then that Peace was taken.

Sue, as might be expected, flew first to the comfort of hysterics, then to the comfort of the bottle. Hannah was of tougher stuff. "Come, Willie, we must go," she said.

Sue was pleading: "What is to become of me, then?"

Hannah turned on her contemptuously. "You are young. You can fight your own battles."

The two women divided the cash in the house, sold everything they could quickly sell—though Sue insisted on keeping the furniture. She had had some recourse to her bottle and was now more cheerful. "I shall find a house and take in lodgers. So I need the furniture," she explained.

It was not long before rumours reached Mr. Smith, the landlord of 5, East Terrace, that something strange was going on. Nobody had been seen about the house. Hurriedly he made his way there. He found the back door swinging open. There was no sign anywhere of the occupiers of the cosy domestic *ménage* that had so impressed him as an honoured guest.

But surely Mr. Thompson would return soon, he thought. After all the old gentleman had forgotten to pay his last quarter's rent. He didn't think Mr. Thompson would fail to do that . . .

CHAPTER SIX

THE MOMENT Peace signed his name to the letter he wrote to Mr. Brion from Newgate Prison, while on remand charged with shooting P.C. Robinson, he virtually signed his own death warrant. Without this link between him and East Terrace and later the treacherous Sue "Thompson" it is difficult to know how he could have been identified as the Banner Cross murderer. His motives in writing the letter are difficult to understand. Perhaps the day-by-day strain of waiting for someone to unmask him was too much, maybe he was still basically so obsessed with Sue that he could go no longer without news of her. To the end he maintained a curious affection for her, though humanly enough he did not hesitate, in his turn, to try to "shop" her.

Sue, having once decided to turn informer, did the job thoroughly. She not only gave away Peace, but helped to track down Mrs. Peace, who had flown north the day after the Blackheath arrest, carrying with her boxes of loot from Evelina Road. Inspector Phillips, of the Metropolitan Police, followed her trail and found her with her daughter and son-in-law at Hazel Road, Darnall, and enough stolen property to stock a small shop. She was charged with receiving, but Hannah kept her nerve and steadily maintained that she had been acting under her husband's orders and was therefore entirely blameless.

The police were desperately anxious to trace the way in which Peace disposed of the enormous quantities of loot which had passed through his hands. They enlisted the aid, not only of Sue, but also of Mr. Brion. Sue left the Longs, with whom she had taken refuge shortly after the home at East Terrace was broken up—she had told them Mr. "Thompson" had left her for another woman—and went to stay with the Brions. During the coming weeks they racked their brains to remember names and addresses let slip by Peace and the police followed up every lead. In the end this secret of Peace's died with him.

Mr. Brion was almost over-zealous in his role of the good citizen. But his position was an unhappy one. He was known to have been closely associated with Mr. "Thompson" for many months, and he seems to have suffered something like guilt by association. He was harassed by newspaper reporters and his neighbours became markedly cool. No doubt he was allowed to overhear little asides about "Birds of a Feather", and "There's no smoke without fire" and so forth.

Any hopes that Peace may have entertained about escaping the consequences of the shooting of Mr. Dyson were dispelled one morning when he was shuffling round the Exercise Yard in Newgate. Standing with the warders was a familiar figure, Police Constable Morris of the Sheffield Police, who had at one time lived near Peace in Darnall and knew him too well to be deceived by the changes in his appearance. He had been sent to London to establish the identity of "Ward" without question so that the legal machinery to bring him back to Sheffield could be set in motion. His "Good morning, Peace," was like a death knell in the prisoner's ears as he shuffled past the little group of officials.

On November 13th the *Daily Telegraph* reported: "It is now established beyond all doubt that the burglar captured by P.C. Robinson is one and the same as the Banner Cross murderer. Numerous articles found in the houses of Peace's relatives have been identified by the owners from whose premises they were stolen during the past two years."

The newspaper also recorded that, in addition to a vast collection of musical instruments found at East Terrace, there had also been found a silver pencil case bearing the inscription "Miss J. A. Peace. Given to her by her beloved Father on her 17th birthday:—

"There is a flower, a gentle flower
That blooms in each shaded spot
And gently to the heart it speaks
Forget me not, Love."

The reporter did not mention that the police had also found that at East Terrace, the writer of these tender lines to his daughter had stowed about the premises in strategic positions a number of firearms, ready to give desperate battle should attempts be made to arrest him.

On November 19th Peace appeared at the Old Bailey on the charge of shooting at Robinson with intent to murder. The Judge was Mr. Justice Hawkins, a man known and feared by the criminal fraternity for the severity of his sentences. Throughout the trial, which was brief, Peace did his best to play the role of a rather enfeebled old man, utterly regretful of his "slip". Indeed his bearing was such that a number of the spectators present were quite unable to believe that such a kindly-looking old man could possibly be concerned in the story unfolded by Robinson and the other policemen. The jury, however, told to hearken to the evidence only, reached a verdict of "Guilty" without even bothering to retire.

Though he could hardly have been expecting otherwise, or perhaps for some other motive, Peace seemed to be overcome by their verdict. Tears streamed down his face, he wrung his hands and gazed wildly about the courtroom as though he could hardly believe his ears. He was asked if he had anything to say, and launched into one of the most amazing tirades ever heard in a British court.

"Yes, I have this to say, my Lord. I have not been fairly dealt with, and I declare before God that I had never any intention to kill. All I meant to do was frighten him, so I might get away. If I'd wanted to kill him I could easily have done it, but I never did. I'd say I didn't fire five shots, I only fired four; and I think I can show you how I can prove only four shots were fired.

"If your Lordship will look at the pistol you'll see it goes off very easily; the sixth barrel went off on its own after I was taken. When the fifth shot went off the policeman had a hold of me and it went off by accident. I really didn't know the pistol was loaded. I hope, My Lord, you will have mercy upon me. I know that I am base and bad. I feel that I am that base and bad that I am neither fit to live nor die. For I have disgraced myself. I have disgraced my friends and I am not fit to live among mankind. I am not fit to meet my God for I am not prepared to do so. So, Oh, My Lord, I know I am base and bad to the uttermost, but I know, at the same time, they have painted my case blacker than it really is. I hope you will take all this into consideration and not pass upon me a sentence of imprisonment that will be the means of my dying in prison, where it is possible that I shall not have the chance among my associates to prepare to meet my God that I hope I shall meet. So, My Lord, do have mercy upon me. I beseech you, give me a chance, My Lord, to regain my freedom and you shall not, with the help of my God, have cause to repent passing a merciful sentence upon me. Oh, My Lord, you yourself expect mercy from the hands of your great and merciful God. Oh, My Lord, do have mercy upon me, a most wretched, miserable man, that man that is not fit to die. I am not fit to live, but with the help of my God I will try to become a good man. I will try to become a man that will be able in the last day to meet my God, my Great Judge, to meet him and to receive the great reward at His Hands for my true repentance. So, Oh, My Lord, have mercy upon me, I pray and beseech you. I will say no more, but, oh, My Lord, have mercy upon me. My Lord have mercy upon me."

Mr. Justice Hawkins then proceeded to sentence Peace to be kept in penal servitude for the rest of his natural life.

Peace collapsed into the arms of the warders in the dock, and the sound of his moaning was heard as he was half-supported, half-carried out of the courtroom to the cells. Once out of sight he is said to have recovered sufficiently to remark to his escort: "Penal servitude for life. It's scandalous. There'll be a petition to the Home Office."

Back in the courtroom the jury asked the Judge that the bravery of Constable Robinson might be recognized and Mr. Justice Hawkins ordered that he be granted £25. In all Robinson made about £300 from his capture of Peace. In addition to the sum awarded at the Old Bailey, he received the outcome of a number of private collections, including £25 from the residents of Blackheath, who also gave him a silver watch and chain. He had earned his rewards. At Pentonville Prison Peace now began the routine, already so familiar to him, of long-term convict. There was nothing more that could be done to bring him to book for the murder of Dyson until Mrs. Dyson could be found. Indeed the whole case against Peace in connection with the Banner Cross killing depended on her, and the Sheffield police had lost trace of her in America. Accordingly Detective Walsh, of the Sheffield police, was sent to America to find her and to try to persuade her to return with him. They had no means of forcing her to do so and without her consent to return there was no hope of convicting Peace.

Despite his own predicament Peace now set about trying to rescue what he could from the wreckage of his life. He was determined to hang on to what property he could—no doubt for the sake of his family rather than himself—and to clear Mrs. Peace of the charge of receiving hanging over her. He asked the Governor of Pentonville if he might send a statement to the Chief Commissioner of Police. Permission was granted and on December 13th the following epistle was forwarded:—

"What I am going to say shall be the truth and nothing but the truth. The property that was at Sheffield at my wife's lodgings I had stolen the greater part of it but things was not stolen I mean the musical instruments for I was a dealer in them and some of them I bought of Mr. Waller (unreadable section here) and some I bought of Mr. Thomas Wilcox's 207 Westminster Bridge Road and I never stole no musical instruments but bought them all.

"Some of these things as been stolen for eighteen months or more so that I could not tell ware they come from without seeing them. some of them come from Blackheath and some from Brixton and some from Dulwich and some from Clapham Common and some from Sydenham and some from around Denmark Hill and if I could see this proprty i could tell ware it all come from and I have not aney person with me when I stole it for I allways went by myself but thear was a box that Mrs. Thompson tooke to Nottingham and left it at her sister, a Mrs. Greagham No 10 North Street, Nottingham and this Mrs. Greagham thinking that her sister Mrs. Thompson would call her self Mrs. Peace has she has been living with me as she thought so that she sade Mrs. Peace ad left home but (unreadable) at the same time Mrs. Thompson and not Mrs. Peace for my wife as not no sisters living.

"My wife was living with me in London at No 5 este terriss everleaner road Nunhead S.E. up to the time of me being taken prisoner and when I stole this proprty I took it home and told my wife that I had bought it at the sales that I was in the habit of atending to buy musical instruments and she did not know that I had stolen them and when I was at Blackheath Police Station I sent a seacted (secret?) mesige out by a man that went out on baile to my wife (Peace must have managed this somehow the first night he was in custody despite close watchfulness by the police) teling her to brake up her home and to go to Sheffield at once and that is how my wife was found at Sheffield with this proprty that i had stolen but she knows nothing of me having stolen it . . ."

Peace had done his best to clear his wife, but his feelings towards Sue "Thompson" were not so friendly. He wrote: "it was Mrs. Thompson that allways sold my thing for me for I dar not do it my self becouse of the £100 that offered by the police for my beentaken prisoner so that Mrs. Thompson was the only person that did now heney thing of my doing and that was the cause of me leting her leive in the same house as me and my wife but my wife did not know nothing of Mrs. Thompson doing this for me."

It was a forlorn hope of revenge on Mrs. "Thompson". When the police offer an informer immunity in return for information to enable them to snare a more important accomplice, they do not go back on their word. They did proceed with their case against Mrs. Peace, but at her trial at the Central Criminal Court early in 1879 the Jury were instructed to find her "Not Guilty" on the grounds that she was a married woman acting under the instructions of her husband.

The Home Secretary was already acquainted with Peace's unique literary style before receiving this document. Earlier Peace had written to him a long diatribe against Mrs. Dyson, alleging that she had been known to threaten her husband's life and saying that he had notes and photographs to prove that she had been carrying on a liaison with him (Peace) in the period before Dyson's death.

Peace was now indeed in a corner for Walsh, the Sheffield policeman, had traced Mrs. Dyson in America and she had immediately volunteered to return to England to give evidence. It says much of her hatred for Peace—whatever their original relationship may have been—that she was prepared to face the ordeal in court she must have known she would have to undergo. She was far too intelligent a woman not to miss the fact that the Defence would attempt to show that her dealings with Peace were suspect, and that, therefore, her eyewitness testimony to her husband's death should be treated with suspicion. On January 7th 1879, she landed back in England and travelled to Sheffield to await Peace's arrival from London to stand trial.

Peace must now have felt he had little to lose and resolved to be as troublesome as he could be. On January 17th he was brought by train from Pentonville to Sheffield for the preliminary hearing of the murder charge. With him were Chief Warder James Crosgrove and Warder William Robertson, who found that the journey came up to their worst expectations. Not only did they have to watch Peace every minute of the way, but he did everything he could to torment them. He had to be hauled, grumbling, along the platform at King's Cross to be put into the special reserved compartment and throughout the journey insisted on getting out at every stop to perform bodily functions.

When the train stopped at Peterborough there was a scene on the platform. Peace had once again insisted on going to the lavatory. He was so long in the recess that the train was signalled away and Robertson had to drag him out, and hustle him back along the platform to the compartment, after throwing a rug around him for decency's sake.

The courtroom of the Sheffield Stipendiary Magistrate, Mr. E. M. E. Welby, was crowded for the hearing. The case had attracted tremendous public interest. Indeed a few days before, Mrs. Dyson, out walking in the town with Detective Walsh, was recognized, and immediately so large a crowd had gathered that they had had to take refuge in a shop and leave by a back exit. Now she sat waiting in court, quietly dressed in widow's black with a veil over her face. She sat apparently quite composed, but it was noticeable that her cheeks were flushed with suppressed emotion.

There was a hush as Peace's name was called and a craning of necks as the little man stepped up into the dock. He looked coolly round the courtroom, giving a friendly nod of recognition towards a number of the police constables on duty whom he knew. He spotted Mrs. Dyson and glared, but she looked composedly back at him.

A *Sheffield and Rotherham Independent* reporter wrote: "How changed his demeanour since I saw him cringing and fawning and pleading for mercy in the Old Bailey. With spectacles on nose, clean shaven and bald head, his features bore an expression that seemed to indicate that he was the injured instead of the injurer."

After Peace's defending solicitor, Mr. William Edwin Clegg, later Sir William Clegg, had unsuccessfully attempted to obtain an adjournment to enable the Defence to go more thoroughly into certain matters, Mrs. Dyson was called into the witness box. She told the story of how her husband had died. She said that when she came out of the closet she had found Peace standing there, pistol in hand. She had screamed and shut herself back in the closet. Her husband had come down the yard to her assistance. She had come out of the closet and seen Peace creeping sideways away towards the exit. As he reached the end of the yard he had fired. The bullet had missed her husband, and Peace fired again. This time her husband had fallen backwards.

The Magistrate said he would adjourn the cross-examination of Mrs. Dyson until the next hearing and the court then heard some other witnesses—and some interjections from Peace, who had sat quietly during Mrs. Dyson's evidence. At one stage Peace interrupted and spoke across the court to the Chief Constable of Sheffield, saying that he objected to a man sitting near the Chief Constable sketching his portrait. He relapsed mumbling when told that the man was a reporter taking notes.

When Mrs. Colgreaves was giving evidence of being taken to Newgate to identify Peace, Peace interrupted at one point, saying "Was I like this?" at the same time twisting his face into a grimace.

The Magistrate: "You had better not interrupt."

Peace: "I beg your pardon, sir, but my life is at stake and I am going to vindicate my character as well as I can. If you don't want me to speak, put a gag in my mouth. When I hear a person perjuring herself I will speak. I wish to say it openly and in Court that up to the time when this woman saw me in Newgate I had disfigured my face so as not to be known. I was not then known as Charles Peace, and I had disfigured my face so that I had deceived all the detectives in London. My face was disfigured when this woman saw me."

Magistrate: "It was merely for your sake I told you not to speak."

Peace: "I am bound to speak when I hear wrong statements."

But he kept quiet for a while until Brassington's story incensed him. Brassington was describing how Peace had tried to force him to read certain letters under the gaslamp in the street shortly before Dyson was shot. "He told me he would make it warm for the strangers before morning. He would shoot them both."

Peace: "Oh, you villain. God reward you. He will".

Brassington also described his visit to Newgate to try to identify Peace. Once again Peace engaged in an argument with the Magistrate, saying: "I am going to have fair play and will interrupt the proceedings to get it." When the Magistrate mildly attempted to explain what the witness had been saying Peace burst out: "I have seen a great deal of injustice done in different courts, but I am not going to have injustice done here."

He continued wrangling about a point in Brassington's story until the Magistrate said: "It is not worth while going into that."

Peace: "Oh yes, but it is worth while to me. I am not a dog. My life is at stake. If you hang me it will only free me from a long dreary life of penal servitude and I don't care much which way it is, but I am going to have full justice done me. I will interrupt you if you do not do justice and, if you gag me, I'll try to interrupt you."

The Prosecuting Solicitor, Mr. Pollard, reminded the Magistrate that if Peace made a nuisance of himself he could be removed from the Court.

The Magistrate: "We have great power, but it is not always wise to exercise it."

At the end of the day of hearing witnesses Peace was remanded until the next Wednesday and his escort prepared to take him back to Pentonville. A huge crowd had gathered outside the courtroom and it was only with difficulty that the police cleared a way for the wagon, with Peace inside, to drive to the railway station. Once clear the wagon was driven at full gallop to the station to avoid the crowd, but a big section of it ran in pursuit, pushed aside the police and crowded the railway platform. Peace and his warders had to push their way through to sit in the waiting-room. When their train came in, police and porters lined up to make a tunnel down which the prisoner and escort could reach their compartment, but the pressure of the crowd was so great that both the convict and the two men, to whom he was linked by handcuffs, were carried off their feet and had literally to struggle their way to the train.

The next Wednesday Crosgrove and Robertson had again to face the task of bringing Peace from Pentonville to Sheffield. This time they were determined to take all precautions to prevent a repetition of the previous journey's behaviour. Peace was heavily manacled, with handcuffs round his wrists. Robertson snapped one bracelet of another pair round the links between Peace's wrists, hanging on to the other bracelet himself. In this way he had full control over Peace's movement.

Peace was again in a truculent mood and demanded to be permitted to pass water frequently. Crosgrove, however, had brought with him a number of bags and he made Peace use these and then throw them out of the carriage window. It was not a pleasant journey but by the time the train was running between Worksop and Sheffield the two warders felt that the worst was over. The train was going fast, about 50 m.p.h., and Peace sat watching through the window as the snow-covered fields he knew so well whizzed past. He had walked over all this ground, both as a hawker, and, no doubt, as a burglar. He knew every inch of it. Suddenly between Shireoaks and Kiveton Park stations he demanded another bag. He stood to use it and then turned to the window to throw the receptacle out.

Robertson stood with him, and just behind him, his arm half round Peace so that with his left hand he could hold the handcuffs snapped round the 'cuffs on Peace's wrists. Suddenly, without any warning of tensed muscles, Peace threw himself forward and dived in a somersault out of the window. The sheer force of his move dragged the handcuffs from Robertson's hands. The warder, however, just managed to grab hold of Peace's left ankle and hung on as hard as he could. Peace was now dangling from the train and he began kicking with all his might at Robertson's hands.

Crosgrove was unable to help his comrade as the window was completely blocked by Robertson's body. He went to the other window and leaning out began pulling at the communication cord. (Trains did not have corridors in those days and the communication cord ran along the top of the outside of the coaches. Unfortunately there was something wrong with the cord and he could not get the alarm bell to sound to warn the train crew. The train raced on, Peace still hanging from it and thrashing wildly with his free foot at the now bleeding and torn hands of Warder Robertson.

Mr. Benjamin Cocker, a Sheffield man, who was in the 1st-class compartment next door, had heard the commotion and he now joined Crosgrove in trying to work the communication cord, but without success. At that moment the train ran through some sidings and both men waved frantically to the signalman on duty in the signal-box. He grinned and waved back in the friendliest manner, without apparently realising that anything was wrong.

Peace had seized the steps to the train with bold hands and was pulling downwards with all his strength. Robertson realised that he was not strong enough to hold Peace much longer and with a last desperate effort wrenched Peace's hands away. As he did so the convict's left boot came off and his twisting, writhing body fell to the side of the track.

At the risk of overbalancing, Crosgrove and Mr. Cocker had now managed to hang on the bell with sufficient force to give the alarm and the train pulled up. The two warders climbed down and set off back to find Peace, but not before Mr. Cocker, with all the assurance of the moneyed Victorian for his social inferiors, had remarked to Robertson, whose hands were dripping with blood: "You are a nice sort of fellow to let that man get out of your grasp."

Crosgrove and Robertson ran back along the track and about a mile away found Peace still lying where he had fallen. Blood was pouring from a head wound, but he was conscious and gave the two men a smile of recognition as they came up. A slow train to Sheffield was coming up the line, and Crosgrove signalled it to stop. Peace was lifted, groaning, into the guard's van, where a rug was thrown over him, and the journey to Sheffield continued.

Afterwards Peace insisted that his leap from the train was intended as a bid to kill himself, and it is true that a piece of paper was found concealed on him, which bore the words: "Bury me at Darnall. Goodbye. God Bless You All". He said: "I knew I could not get away. My hope was that I would be cut to pieces under the wheels and then buried at Darnall". It is more likely that, in fact, he had decided on one last gamble for liberty. If he was killed, at least he would have cheated the hangman; if not, there was a desperate chance he might get across the fields to Darnall, where friends and relatives would help him to escape. He probably owed his life to Warder Robertson. That bulldog-spirited officer's last heave to pull him back had swung him round in such a way that, as he fell, his head hit the train step, knocking him out so that it was a limp body that fell in the snow.

In Sheffield a crowd of several thousands was waiting in the bitter cold outside the Town Hall to see Peace arrive. The Chief Constable had sent a party of policemen to escort Peace from the station. When the train drew in, revealing an empty reserved compartment, now containing only the warders' cutlasses, the news spread through the city that Peace had escaped. The crowd before the Town Hall became so excited that the Chief Constable, Mr. Jackson, had to address it from an upstairs window. He told them it was true that Peace had escaped—at which there was a groan from the crowd—but he had now been recaptured. At this there was a tremendous burst of cheering.

When the slow train arrived at the station Peace, groaning and complaining of cold, was carried to a waiting police van and driven to the police station in Water Lane. Here he was given medical attention, including a large dose of brandy and milk, and allowed to curl up in a pile of rugs to sleep. His vitality was enormous, for though he complained that he was dying, a warder watching him during the night saw him peeping stealthily from his nest of rugs to see if he might risk a movement.

The next morning he objected to the milk and brandy which the police surgeon had ordered he should drink, though he said he did not mind if it was whisky. However, the surgeon had issued his orders and the warders forced it down, despite Peace's cries of "murder". He was determined to wrest the maximum amount of concessions for his injuries and he groaned and complained of the cold constantly.

The Prosecution were determined that, if possible, Peace should be tried at the next Assizes, which were due to begin at Leeds in a few days' time, and, if this was to be effected, the preliminary hearing must be completed. Accordingly it was decided that the hearing must be resumed on Friday, January 24th. Peace could not be brought into court so the hearing was held in the corridor outside his cell. A table and chairs were put in for the use of officials and witnesses. The corridor was long and narrow and the only light filtered in through a double-grated window at one end. It was a dark winter's day and candles were lit. Peace was brought from his cell, groaning: "It is not justice. Not proper", and placed in an armchair and wrapped round with rugs.

He gazed round vacantly and asked: "What are we here for?"

The Stipendiary: "This is the preliminary inquiry, which is being proceeded with, after being adjourned."

Peace: "I am not able to bear it. I ought not to be brought here." He kept a running fire of complaints: "I am very cold", "This is not justice", over and over again, but the main tenor of his worry was at all costs to secure another remand. However, ignoring the muttered interjections from the huddled figure in the armchair, his bloodshot eyes winking out from under the bandages, the cross-examination of Mrs. Dyson was begun. Throughout its long length Peace never took his eyes from her. Once he half-rose from his chair, pointed at her, his eyes alight with malign hatred of the woman, who in steady, but clearly audible tones, told the story that could hang him.

When she described how Peace had threatened her husband, he muttered "Go on, lass, go on, Thou art getting along nicely." Another time he began saying loudly that he had "lots of witnesses to prove that base bad woman has threatened my life, and threatened her husband's life", then he fell back. "I cannot talk. I am too bad." It did not stop him from continual interrupting. In the light of the candles, flickering in the draughts, Mrs. Dyson's face was quite without emotion.

The Defence had only one hope for Peace. They must cast serious doubt on Mrs. Dyson's version of the relationship with Peace and seek to show that Peace had shot Dyson in the course of a struggle. They were able to do neither. Many years later Peace's solicitor, Mr. Clegg, wrote: "Mrs. Dyson was a remarkably clever woman and, speaking from my own experience, in over 50 years in connection with criminal matters I have no hesitation in saying that she was one of the cleverest women witnesses I ever met. I believe myself that although the woman denied it there was some association between her and Peace, to what extent I don't know. I am quite certain the letters and scraps of paper were written by her to Peace. She denied it and just as I was getting to the serious point she fell back on the well-known trick of witnesses who have got into difficulties—loss of memory."

The letters to which Mr. Clegg referred were those found in a bundle dropped by Peace while escaping from Banner Cross the night he shot Dyson. The letters were certainly of a type likely to have been written by a woman to a secret lover. One read—:

"How well you never told that man I looked at you out of the window you left me to find out for myself and would not put me on my guard as I do you. Hope you won't do it again. Don't talk to little Willie much, or give him any halfpennies. Don't be a fool. It looks as if you want people to know the way (illegible) If you are not more careful we will have to say quits. I have told you not to say anything until."

Another: —"Saturday afternoon. I write these few lines to thank you for all your kindness which I shall never forget, from you and your wife. She is a good one. Does she know you are to give me things or not. How can you keep them concealed? One thing I wish you to do is to frame his mother's photograph and send it in with my music book. If you please do it when he is in. Many thanks for your kind advice. I hope I shall benefit by it. I shall try to do right to everyone if I can, for I can always look upon you as a friend. Goodbye. I have not much time. Burn this when you have read it."

On a piece of torn paper: "Give it to me up in the garret, but don't talk for fear he is not going only his sister is coming love to all."

Also on a piece of paper: "Things are very bad for peple told him everything. Do keep quiet and dont let anyone see you. Money send me some."

Peace had kept up his interruptions throughout and when Mrs. Dyson's evidence was being read over he put his head on the table and began moaning. He then drew a rug over his head, but continued to make such an uproar from beneath it that a warder pulled it off his head and told him to keep quiet. He was determined, however, to make the maximum amount of difficulty to all concerned, cutting across his own Solicitor, demanding to call witnesses and repeating that Mrs. Dyson had threatened his life. "She has pointed pistols and things at me."

After the Magistrate had told him that he was committed for trial, he whined: "Will you let me sit before the fire a bit before I go. I am really very bad."

The Chief Constable pointed out that he would be warm enough in his cell, it was the draughts that made the corridor cold. "You can put me in irons if you like, but put me near a fire," Peace persisted.

Despite his protests he was removed, cursing and groaning, to his cell, where he saw Mr. Clegg and discussed the hearing with great clarity of understanding. Indeed that evening he was in excellent spirits, chaffing his warders, referring jocularly to his escape and generally boasting about his exploits. The next morning he ate a hearty breakfast. However, later that day when Inspector Bradbury came to take him to Wakefield Prison, where he was to stay until the trial, he insisted he was too weak to walk and the warders carried him from his cell, laid him on a mattress in the police van, from there to a mattress in the guard's van of the train and at Wakefield carried him on a stretcher to the prison. Once in the prison he encountered a warder who told him to "stow his nonsense" and he walked quite steadily to his cell.

After some days in Wakefield Peace was again removed to Armley Prison, near Leeds, where he was due to appear at the January Assizes. From both Wakefield and Leeds he poured out a steady stream of letters to his family and to Sue, to whom he wrote asking for goods left at Peckham to be sold to help pay for his defence. There seems little doubt that a number of the letters were written with the idea that they should be sold for publication. The newspapers were competing keenly for the slightest scraps of information about Peace and substantial sums of money passed into the hands of the Peace family for such material.

It seems very likely that a number of reporters actually managed to see Peace himself while he was awaiting trial, for several newspapers carried long interviews—ostensibly with "old pals"—which gave points of detail that could only have been known to Peace himself. The pace became so hot that finally the managing editor of one newspaper, piqued by the success of his rivals, wrote to the Home Secretary complaining that certain reporters were paying out three-figure sums for "exclusive" material from Peace's relatives, and were even accompanying relatives on visits to the convict.

Forwarded to the Home Secretary with this complaint was a cutting from a Sheffield newspaper, describing a conversation between Peace and his stepson Willie in a way that certainly suggests a skilled shorthand writer was present. It quoted such scraps of conversation between the two men as:—

Peace: "Have you asked those men at Darnall who were intimate with— (presumably Mrs. Dyson though the newspaper was too discreet to name her) to come forward in my defence?"

Willie: "I have asked them, but they will not come forward." and later:—

Willie: "There are plenty of witnesses to speak that Mrs. Dyson has not told the truth and if she has sworn false in one thing they did not ought to take her evidence in another. It ought to be thrown out altogether."

Peace (with much bitterness): "You are right. That is justice, but it is not Law."

Eventually the Home Secretary was harried into ordering the Governor at Armley Prison to investigate the suggestions of corruption among his own staff. The Governor wrote to the Home Office exonerating his own men, but saying it was true that newspapermen were paying large sums of money to Peace's relatives, who were engaged in manufacturing a variety of stories to satisfy the demand.

On February 3rd Peace was taken to Leeds Town Hall where he was put in a cell overnight, appearing for his trial the next day. He was half-carried, half-supported into the dock in the crowded Crown Court, where he pleaded "Not Guilty" to the charge of murdering Arthur Dyson. Perhaps by this time he had abandoned all hope of escaping for throughout the trial, conducted by Mr. Justice Lopes, he sat quite quietly in the dock. He made no outbursts, though he was heard to mutter angrily once or twice when evidence was being given. Once he muttered an aside to the warders while Mrs. Dyson was giving evidence that caused even those iron-faced men to hide their laughter behind their hands. But mostly he sat, white-faced, a motionless figure in broad-arrow convict garb, only his restless eyes, moving from witness to judge, from judge to counsel, from counsel to jury, indicating that his sharp wits were still active.

Peace's own Counsel, Mr. (later Sir) Frank Lockwood, fought a magnificent battle for his life. There was only one slender hope, and that was to discredit Mrs. Dyson, firstly by forcing her to admit a closer intimacy with Peace than she had hitherto confessed, and secondly to drag from her an admission that Peace had shot Dyson during the course of a struggle.

In view of Mrs. Dyson's answers in court, and her subsequent statements in public, Lockwood's Brief from Sir William Clegg, which is still in existence, is an interesting document, though it must be read in the light that Clegg was, of course, setting out everything of aid to his client. Much of the Brief was devoted to examining the packet of letters dropped by Peace at Banner Cross at the time of the murder of Dyson and which Mrs. Dyson had continued to deny writing.

Clegg wrote: "She (Mrs. Dyson) admits that the prisoner gave her a ring, and states that she does not know whether any person besides herself and the prisoner knew about the ring. She thinks perhaps the prisoner's daughter did. She denies that the writing (of the letters) is hers, but it is a remarkable fact that, if she and the prisoner were the only two persons who knew about the ring, anybody else should write the letter the contents of which are somewhat remarkable as the letter stated 'that r——g fits the little finger. Many thanks. Love to Janey (the prisoner's daughter)'. It is hardly likely that it is the daughter because it requires a strong stretch of the imagination to believe that she would send her love to herself and would state that the ring fitted because there is a great difference between the two, Mrs. Dyson being a stout woman and the prisoner's daughter a meagre little woman."

Referring to the letter which read: "Mrs. Norton is raising hell about what I——(unreadable) could you settle it and send me a pint that is I love and——(unreadable) to let me have a pint," Sir William told the Counsel:—

"The Mrs. Norton was the landlady of the Halfway House at Darnall. The witness (Mrs. Dyson) says she remembers the name. Mrs. Norton is now married and is called Liversedge and is a client of the prisoner's solicitors and she had informed them that she knew Mrs. Dyson who used to come for drink and stay drinking, not only with the prisoner, but with other men as well and that once she had her face blacked (?) and had to be put out by Mrs. Liversedge as she was drunk.

"Mrs. Liversedge also says that she has let her have drink on the credit of the prisoner and which he has paid for. Mrs. Liversedge adds that the prisoner owes her for two quarts supplied to Mrs. Dyson, supplied to her just before the quarrel, and in consequence Peace told her not to let Mrs. Dyson have any more."

Of Mrs. Dyson the Brief says: "It is a notorious fact in the neighbourhood where she lived that she was a drunkard and would do anything for drinks."

With regard to the way in which the notes were supposed to have been passed to Peace (of which much was to be made at the trial) Clegg said that a man named Kirkham had stated that not only had he taken notes on several occasions from Mrs. Dyson to Peace, but had also taken notes from Peace and given them to Mrs. Dyson.

The Defence version of the actual shooting was set out. "The prisoner says that when Dyson appeared on the scene, the prisoner seeing he could not get away from him, turned round and having a revolver with him, said if he moved he would fire. Dyson did not stop and the prisoner fired and shot over his head. Before the prisoner could get away the deceased got hold of him and they had a struggle and both got on the floor and whilst scuffling on the floor (the prisoner underneath) the pistol went off accidentally and shot the deceased in the left temple."

Perhaps the most startling information in the Brief is the statement: "We have also heard on very good authority and which is to be relied upon that the prisoner and the witness (Mrs. Dyson) were at the Fair at Sheffield together *the day before* the murder and whilst there went in a show belonging to a person named Charles Turner, then to the Norfolk Hotel opposite from there, then to Milner's Star Concert Room and then to Turner's Vaults, High Street. They were together all the afternoon and from Sheffield went together to the Stag Hotel (this information from the landlady of the hotel who knows Mrs. Dyson very well), having Mrs. Dyson's little boy with them."

It is one of the oddest aspects of the whole affair that there is a suggestion that Mrs. Dyson took her little boy with her to a clandestine meeting with her lover. One wonders, indeed, just what role this little boy played throughout. Mrs. Dyson seems to have been a devoted mother and a woman who was fond of children. Her son must have needed her constant attention. How—if she was carrying on at any time an affair with Peace—did she persuade the lad not to tell his father of outings and excursions with their neighbour? Was this little boy "the good authority" to which Clegg refers in his Brief?

The whole truth of the relationships between Peace and Mrs. Dyson—whatever it was—remained locked within the mind of this formidable woman.

Lockwood took advantage of every opening his instructing solicitors had given him, but he never shook the calm of Mrs. Dyson. She refused to sit to give her evidence and stood firmly, without showing any emotion, throughout his gruelling cross-examination. Lockwood forced her hard on every point, but she would not yield.

She said that, when she had come out of the closet in the yard to find Peace outside, his pistol in his hand, he had said: "Speak or I'll fire", and she had stepped back into the closet and locked herself in. She had screamed and a moment later heard her husband coming down the yard. She had then stepped out of the closet and seen Peace making off, with her husband behind him. Peace had turned round and fired, the bullet striking the wall. He had fired again and her husband had fallen.

Cross-examined by Lockwood she said: "I am prepared to swear my husband never touched the prisoner before the shots were fired."

However, she did agree that her husband had fallen on his back, an important point in Lockwood's case that there had been a fight, for the tendency when a man is shot as Dyson was shot is for the victim to fall forwards.

"I will swear that my husband did not get hold of the prisoner," she persisted, "he did not catch hold of the prisoner's arm, which held the revolver, and the prisoner did not strike my husband on the chin and nose."

Failing to shake her on this point Lockwood turned to the story of her relationship with Peace. Mrs. Dyson said that her husband had begun to dislike Peace in the spring of 1876.

Was he jealous? No.

Do you remember showing your husband a photo of yourself and the prisoner? Yes, it was taken at the Sheffield Fair.

How came you to be photographed together?—We went to the Fair with some children. The children were photographed, but we were in a separate picture. I cannot say whether it was the Summer or Winter fair.

Lockwood then handed up to her two letters from the bundle which had been found in the field at Banner Cross the day after the shooting. Questioned about one of them, Mrs. Dyson denied that she had written: "Don't let him see anything if you meet me in the Wicker. Hope nothing will turn up to prevent it. Love to Janie."

Do you remember the prisoner giving you a ring?—Yes. I threw it away. The ring did not fit me.

Did you ever write this: "I do not know what train I shall go by for I have a good deal to do this morning. Will see as soon as I can. I think it will be easier after you leave. He won't watch so. The ring fits the little finger. Many thanks. Love to Janey. I will tell you what I think of, when I see you about arranging matters, if it will. Excuse the scribble." Now did you write that?—No.

Mrs. Dyson did admit that she had been to a public-house with Peace on one occasion, but when Lockwood called a series of people into court, she gradually and unwillingly agreed that she had visited places of entertainment with Peace "once or twice, but not more often".

Have you ever been to the "Star" music hall with Peace?—I don't know it by that name.

Have you been to any music hall with Peace?—I have been to a place where there is a picture gallery, and where it looked as if singing went on. There was a small stage and tables and chairs.

Have you been three or four times to the music hall in Spring street?—No, I have been only once. I know a public house at Darnall called "The Halfway House". To my knowledge I have never had drink there which was put down to Peace.

That won't do. Are you prepared to swear that you have not had drink there on Peace's credit?—Never to my knowledge.

I have shown you some letters—have you written a letter to the prisoner?—No.

Do you know a little girl named Elizabeth Hutton?

At this point a girl, about nine was brought into court.

Can you swear you have never sent that child with a note to Peace?—Not with a note.

What did you send her with?—I sent her with receipts for some pictures which the prisoner had framed. He was in the habit of asking my husband to write out his receipts and letters.

Now look at that child again. Will you swear that child has not brought back notes from Peace to you?—She brought me one, and I returned it.

Next Lockwood turned his attention to the night *before* Dyson was shot. "Were you," he asked Mrs. Dyson, "at the Stag Hotel, Sharrow?" Mrs. Dyson said she had been with her neighbour, Mrs. Padmore's little boy of six years old.

Was anyone else with you?—No.

At this point Mrs. Redfern, the landlady of the hotel, was brought into court and Lockwood, raising his voice, again asked Mrs. Dyson if she had been alone that night. Mrs. Dyson then said: "A man followed me in and sat down beside me."

Was the man the prisoner?—No.

Will you swear that?—I would almost swear the prisoner was not the man.

That will not do. On your oath, did not this man go into "The Stag" with you that night—No, he did not.

Did he not follow you in?—I don't know that he did, unless he made himself different from what he is now.

What did you mean by saying that you would almost

swear he was not the man?—Because he was so much in the habit of disguising himself.

Did you speak to the man?—I don't remember.

Did he speak to you?—He asked me where I had been, or where I was going, or something of that kind.

Did you answer him?—Yes, I passed some remark.

Did the man go out when you went out?—Yes, he followed me out.

Do you mean to say, on oath, that you did not see the prisoner and that he did not tell you he would come to see you the next night?—No, he did not.

Remorselessly Lockwood ground on with his questions seeking to prove that Mrs. Dyson had been conducting an affair with Peace right up to the time of her husband's death. Mrs. Dyson went on denying it in a clear, level voice, her face betraying no sign of strain or embarrassment. Lockwood had the landlady of the "Halfway House" hotel brought into court.

Have you ever been turned out of that house on account of being drunk?—No.

What! Never?—I have never been drunk in my life.

Will you swear this?—Yes.

Lockwood pointed at the landlady of the public house. "Will you swear you have never been drunk in this woman's house?"

Mrs. Dyson admitted that she might have been "slightly inebriated".

Will you swear you have never been turned out of the house for being "slightly inebriated"?—No, not to my knowledge.

Quite true. You might not have been aware of it.

The Defending Counsel went on fighting, but his attempt to show that there had been a fight before Dyson died was badly shaken by the evidence of Dr. Harrison, the surgeon called to the scene. The Doctor agreed that Dyson had had some slight abrasions on the nose and chin, but added: "I do not think they were caused by a fist". He did not think a fist would have produced the effect, not even if there had been a ring on the finger. The abrasions seemed to be caused by sand. He thought that they were caused by Dyson hitting his face lightly against the wall during his fall.

Lockwood fought on. He made a powerful and lengthy appeal to the jury, which he opened by saying that throughout the country there had been "a wild and merciless cry for blood". The Press, in their search for news about Peace, had not hesitated to prejudice the man's life—a remark which elicited from Peace a rousing "Hear hear". The whole case, said Lockwood, depended on Mrs. Dyson. Were the jury prepared to condemn a man to die on the testimony of that woman?

Mr. Justice Lopes, in his summing up, said that the Defence had put forward the theory that Peace and Dyson had fought and that the first shot was fired to frighten Dyson away, and the second had gone off by accident. If that was the opinion of the jury, they must find Peace guilty of manslaughter, not murder. "It is important to remember, however, that it is only a theory and not supported by a particle of evidence."

It was a quarter past seven in the evening when the jury retired to consider their verdict. They were not gone long. Ten minutes later they filed back into their box and Peace stood forward in the front of the dock. The gaslight threw dark shadows and it was impossible to see any expression on that strange mobile face. He did not flinch when the Foreman of the jury announced that he had been found "Guilty" of murdering Dyson. He was asked if he had anything to say. His shoulder shrugged slightly. "It's no use my saying anything." His voice was faint, but perfectly controlled.

He stood quite still as Mr. Justice Lopes, holding the small black square of the cap, which was until recently placed upon a Judge's white wig when sentence of death was passed, implored him "during the short time that may remain to you to live" to prepare himself for eternity.

Then the Judge's hand went up to fit the black cap upon his head and he spoke the words that Peace had heard spoken to young William Habron:— "The sentence is that you be taken from this place to the place from whence you came and thence to the place of execution and that you be there hanged by the neck until you are dead; and that your body be buried within the precincts of the prison in which you shall have been last confined. And may the Lord have mercy upon your soul."

Peace was guided down the steps from the dock, where he was handcuffed and leg irons were snapped on. He walked along the corridor towards the gate where the prison van was waiting to collect him. He was muttering to himself as he went. As he paused for a moment for the gate to be opened he turned to his escort and remarked: "I am going to be executed and what I say is this, I am going to be hung for something I done, but never intended."

Back in Armley Prison he was given his dinner, which he ate with a hearty appetite and he then wrote letters to his solicitor, Mr. Clegg, and to Frank Lockwood, thanking them for their efforts on his behalf. He sent Lockwood his finger-ring, a massive circlet of metal like a knuckleduster and without doubt designed for that purpose, as a memento.

The cell in which Peace was to spend the rest of his life was on the ground floor of the prison. The only exterior light came from two small slits in the wall and the gas was lit night and day. The space had been divided in half by an inner railing of steel bars from floor to ceiling so that anyone entering the cell door saw a kind of cage in which Peace's bed and table and chairs were set. He was watched with unceasing vigilance, for on January 28th the Director of the C.I.D. of Great Scotland Yard had written to the Director of Convict Prisons:—

"I have the honour to acquaint you that information has been received by the police that efforts will be made by the relatives and friends of the convict Peace to prevent his being executed, should he be found guilty of murder, by conveying poison to him in order that he may commit suicide. It is stated that the convict has previously made arrangements with his friends that, if at any time he should be condemned to death, they were to visit him and carry with them in their mouths poison wrapped in tinfoil which was to be passed to him in the act of kissing."

On February 4th, the Director of the C.I.D. again wrote to the Director of Prisons saying that he was unable to obtain confirmation "in repudiation of the caution given by Mrs. Thompson, the late mistress of the convict Peace, as to the mode in which he would attempt suicide. Mrs. Thompson is frequently in a state of intoxication and the public excitement the case has aroused has not had a satisfactory influence on the persons connected with the convict who outdo each other in the grossness of their fabrications. I transmit the information and take the liberty of suggesting it will not be difficult to frustrate such communication of poison without absolutely forbidding a condemned man to embrace his wife and daughter."

The Governor of the prison reported to the Home Office: "Every possible precaution is being taken. I have selected the most trustworthy officers to guard Peace both night and day and they are visited frequently by myself and the Chief Warder. The convict, when occupying his bed, which is placed in the middle of the condemned cell, has a warder sitting on either side, close watching. When sitting up at the table (which is a fixture) the same plan is followed and when walking about the cell the officers accompany him on either side.

"No relatives will be allowed inside the inner railing and gate of the condemned cell and the convict is not allowed to be seated nearer than six feet of such railing. No letters are allowed to be handled by him, such being read to him as often as he wishes by myself or the Chief Warder. The convict is a most artful and cunning man and my orders must be strictly carried out."

Acknowledging this communication, Mr. R. C. Anderson, Secretary to the Prison Commission, wrote: "You are to carry out generally the necessary guarding and watching with as little annoyance to the prisoner as possible and compatible with all fair precautions."

It was agreed that Peace must be permitted to talk to the Prison Chaplain alone, though two warders were to stand watch outside the cell door and ready to answer any call for assistance from the Chaplain. Peace also asked for his spectacles and, after some consideration, it was decided to let him have the use of a pair, made from horn so that he could not use them to injure himself, and when he was not actually wearing them they were to be put outside the cell.

Peace, in fact, gave the prison authorities no trouble. He spent most of his time writing letters to relatives and reading devotional works. He seemed worried about the state of the souls of those guarding him and exhorted his warders to live the good life and prepare their souls for death.

He seemed certain that his own death would find him prepared. He wrote to his family: "I know there is a merciful God, whom I have sinned against and broken all his commandments all the days of my life." He said that he drew comfort from thinking that if he had not been sentenced to death he would have had to spend all the rest of his life in prison and would thus have died "surrounded by a class of men anything but good and god-fearing." He prayed each day with the prison chaplain, the Rev. Oswald Cookson, and during one of their talks together Peace asked the clergyman rhetorically: "What is the scaffold?" and answered himself: "A short cut to Heaven."

He received visitors constantly, among the first being his daughter and her newly-born baby. "Let me look at it", Peace asked, so Mrs. Bolsover held up the child to the bars for him to get a closer look. Peace gazed at his grandchild for a moment and then said: "God in Heaven bless its little soul". He asked how Mrs. Peace was faring and was told that she was not well and "in poor spirits", but would be coming to see him.

There was to be some trouble before this could be effected. He had earlier received a letter from Sue Thompson asking if she might visit him in prison. Peace had written back:—

"My poor Sue,

I receive your letter today and I have my kind governor's permission for you to come and see me at once so come up to the prison and bring this letter with you and you will get to see me. I do particularly wish to see you it is my wish that you will obey me in this one thing for you have obeyed me in many thing but do obey me in this one. Do not let this letter fall into the hands of the press. Hoping to see you at once I remane yours ever well wisher Charles Peace."

Mrs. Peace got to hear of this proposed visit and via Mr. and Mrs. Bolsover conveyed the message to her husband that if Mrs. Thompson was allowed to visit him, she would not. Peace told his son-in-law and daughter that his only interest now in seeing his Sue was to persuade her to give up drink and live a new life. Mrs. Peace remained adamant. So when Sue arrived at the prison she was told that under no circumstances would she be allowed to see Peace. She remained in lodgings near the prison until after the execution and made several attempts to see her former lover, but without avail.

She wrote pathetically:—

"My own Dear Jack,

What do you mean by turning against me. I who have cared for you. What must I believe. Hannah is admitted to see you as your wife and you have most solemnly sworn that she was not. When you and I went to Hull you told me you would and should marry me. Oh why am I to suffer this. I am prevented from seeing you and am pointed at in the streets. Have I deserved this. You would not have gone out had you taken my advice upon the 9th of October. It is most terrible I am not allowed to see you . . . John, darling I must see you once again upon this earth. Darling, remember the last time I saw you. You turned back a second time to kiss me. Oh, I do implore you upon my knees to see me . . ."

At the time when she was attempting to persuade Peace to see her Sue was also in correspondence with the Home Office in respect of her claim for the £100 reward money for betraying him. Finally on May 8th, months after Peace's death, she was granted the reward and then faded into obscurity. She received offers to appear at music halls and beer gardens as the lover of the notorious Charlie Peace, but she decided to reject them.

She had become a gaunt woman, whose wandering eye and twitching hands bore testimony to the ordeal through which she had passed—and her means to cope with it. She told a reporter: "I have my own character to redeem, and if I have my health and strength I hope to do it." In view of the fact that the reporter noted that, when offered refreshment, she "partook of steak and onions, rinsed down with brandy and water", one wonders to what end Sue came in the byways of Victorian back streets where drunkenness and a wayward, feckless character led only too inexorably to degradation.

It is doubtful if her friendship with the Brions survived the granting of the reward money, for Mr. Brion himself hopefully put in a claim. He was entitled to something for his trouble. He and Mrs. Brion had dashed about the countryside following up leads supplied by Sue as to the whereabouts of stolen property and they managed to recover certain stolen items for the police. Though the police were aware that Mr. Brion was an innocent victim of Peace's charm, the neighbours at Peckham took no such kindly view. The couple found themselves shunned and the target of rumours to the effect that anyone who had spent so much time with Peace must, by association, be a criminal as well.

A few days before Peace was due to be executed Brion travelled to Leeds and was permitted to see him. Brion explained his difficulty to his former inventor-colleague and Peace assured him that he would do all he could to help. He wrote a letter to Brion which read: "I do truly say that neither you, nor any other friend or neighbour within miles of Nunhead and Peckham did know anything of what I was doing of, for I always represented myself as an independent man, and also was very careful about going out and coming in, so that I know there was no suspicion of me. As for you, Mr. Brion, you might have lived in my house along with me and I should not have let you know anything. So that I am very sorry to think that the people round Peckham Rye should so most wrongfully affect an innocent man's character by connecting it with one of the worst men this world ever produced."

Peace's generosity went further. He drew up a Deed of Gift: "I, Charles Peace, freely and without cost, herewith of my own accord give to Mr. H. Brion my inventions as follows:—

"Invention for supplying members of fire brigades and others with pure air when buildings are on fire.

"Improved brush for washing railway carriages, etc.

"Hydraulic tank for supply of water."

The details of the last invention are lost to us. It maybe referred to the famous scheme for raising sunken ships by pumping in air, for, in the course of their work, the two men had built a large tank in which they sank and raised a specially constructed toy boat.

In the main Peace's visitors were his many relatives. On occasions no fewer than thirteen would turn up at once and the Governor insisted that they be divided into parties to go into the cell. Here they found Peace sitting in a wooden armchair, with two warders on either side. He presented a ghastly appearance, for he was undoubtedly suffering from the effects of his ordeal, and reaction from his jump from the train. He complained that his head was bad and it was heavily bandaged.

Peace seemed overcome with emotion at the sight of his relatives and told them his only purpose now was to make a good death. He exhorted them, particularly his brother Dan, to profit by his own example and from then on to lead god-fearing lives.

Finally Mrs. Peace agreed to visit him and travelled from Sheffield with her son, Willie, and a nephew, Thomas Neil. Peace appeared overjoyed to see her and they talked for over an hour. He explained that he was too weak to walk alone, but his mind was clear and he had in his cell a Bible and Prayer Book and tracts sent to him by a number of well-wishers. He proceeded to demonstrate his alertness of mind by giving Mrs. Peace a long list of instructions as to how she might most usefully dispose of properties held by her and not claimed by the police as stolen property.

Contemporary press reports claim that, when they parted, Peace pressed on his wife his gold spectacles as being the only personal possessions he could give her as a keepsake. It is possible that the Governor, while not allowing Peace to have the spectacles for his own use, did permit him to have them for this brief time to make this gesture to his wife.

When not seeing visitors, talking to the Chaplain, the Rev. Oswald Cookson, or prison officials, Peace spent most of the last days of his life writing letters, or studying his Bible. He seemed early to have abandoned any hope of a reprieve, though a number of people wrote to the Home Office asking for his life to be spared for a variety of humanitarian and religious reasons.

It is doubtful if he would have cared to have been spared on the terms suggested by Mr. O. Brant, of Oxford, who wrote to the Home Secretary: "The wretched man Peace will be hanged, but will hanging be a deterrent to others. I fear not. He will soon be forgotten and perhaps copied by others. Why should he not have a reprieve for a time and be publicly flogged once in every two months as near to the place of his murders as possible.

"I am quite certain more public floggings with the CAT would greatly trend to the suppression of murder, wife beating and drunkenness."

The date for the execution was February 25th and on the 17th Peace asked if he might see the Rev. Littlewood, his old friend, the Vicar of Darnall. On the 19th Mr. Littlewood was shown into the Condemned Cell, where Peace was eagerly waiting.

What followed was later the subject of a remarkable account in *The Sheffield Daily Telegraph*, presumably dictated by Mr. Littlewood himself. The accuracy of what was said was due to the fact that large parts of Peace's confession were written down by Mr. Littlewood at the time, a unique document in criminal history. Years later Mr. Littlewood's relatives attempted to find this document, but could not do so. Mrs. H. Walker, the Vicar's daughter, told me she had searched everywhere for it, but believed her father had destroyed it because he did not wish it ever to come on the market as a souvenir.

Peace is reported to have said to Mr. Littlewood before beginning his confession: "You know, sir, I have nothing to gain and nothing to lose in my present position. I know I will be hanged next Tuesday. I desire to be hanged. I do not want to linger out my life in penal servitude. I would rather end my days on Tuesday than have that dreadful looking forward to all those years but I do want as far as I can to atone in some measure for the past by telling all I know to someone in whom I have confidence."

Parts of the confession have already been given in this volume in relation to the Habron trial, and with reference to the Sunday school clock. After speaking of this latter Peace went on:—

"Now, Mr. Littlewood, about the Banner Cross murder. I want first to say solemnly before you in the sight of these men (the warders) and in the hearing of God that several witnesses grossly perjured themselves. Brassington and Mrs. Padmore were two. I freely and fully forgive them, and hope to meet them in Heaven. You may ask me what their perjury was. Well, they swore that they heard me threaten Mrs. Dyson. That is a lie. I call to God to witness that I never did threaten Mrs. Dyson. I tell you, sir, that Mrs. Dyson and I were on such intimate terms that I could not have done so. It would not have suited my purpose to have quarrelled with, or threatened Mrs. Dyson.

Peace then told the full story of the Whalley Range murder, but afterwards went on "I came to Sheffield the night after the (Habron) trial and went to Banner Cross in the evening. (Presumably of the next day.) I wanted to see Mrs. Dyson. I stood on the low wall at the back of the house. I knew the house very well, both back and front, and I knew the bedroom was at the back. While I was standing I noticed a light in the bedroom. The blind was up and I could plainly see Mrs. Dyson carrying a candle and moving about the room.

"I watched her for some time and I then saw that she was putting her boy to bed. I then 'flipped my fingers' and gave a sort of subdued whistle to attract the attention of Mrs. Dyson as I had often done before at other places. I had not long to wait. Mrs. Dyson came downstairs—she had evidently heard the signal and knew I was there—and in response to my call she came out and passed out to the closet. I then got down off the wall and went towards the closet. I was with her some time. You may ask what I wanted to do with her there. Well, I did not do what people think. I went simply for the purpose of begging her to induce her husband to withdraw the warrant which had been issued against me. I was tired of being hunted about, not being able to come and go as I liked. I only wanted the warrant withdrawn. That was my only object and if I had got that done I should have gone away again.

"Mrs. Dyson became very noisy and defiant, used fearful language and threats against me and I got angry. Taking my revolver out of my pocket I held it up to her face and said, 'Now be careful what you are saying to me. You know me of old, and know what I can do. You know I am not a man to be talked to in that way. If there is one man who will not be trifled with by you, or anybody else, it is Charles Peace.'

"She did not take warning, but continued to use threats against me and angered me. I tried to keep as cool as I could. While these angry words were going on Mr. Dyson hastily made his appearance. As soon as I saw Mr. Dyson I immediately started to go down the passage which leads to the main road. I was not sharp enough. Mr. Dyson seized me before I could get past him. I told him to stand back and let me go, but he did not and then I fired one barrel of my revolver wide at him to frighten him, expecting that he would then loose me and that I should get off. He got hold of the arm to which I had strapped my revolver, which I always did, and I then knew I had not a moment to spare. I made a desperate effort, wrenched the arm from him and fired.

"It was a life or death struggle, Mr. Littlewood, but even then I did not intend to shoot Mr. Dyson. This you must remember—my blood was up. I had been angry at what that woman had said to me. I had only come to ask what I thought I should get and I would have gone away and not troubled them again, but then Mr. Dyson struggling with me, and having fired one shot, I knew if I was captured it would mean transportation for life. That was what made me determined to get off somehow. I fired again, but with no intention of killing him. I saw Dyson fall. I did not know where he was hit, nor had any idea that it was such a wound as would prove fatal. All that was in my head at the time was to get away and if he had not so obstinately prevented me I should have got away.

"I assure you, sir, I never did intend, either there, or anywhere else, to take a man's life. But I was determined that I should not be caught at that time, as the result, knowing what I had done before, would have been worse even than had I stayed under the warrant. After firing the first shot I knew then how serious it was, and whatsoever was sworn at the trial, I tell you that we had a scuffle, that it was a life and death struggle and for a time Dyson had the best of it.

"With my revolver I could have shot him dead at the first, but I did not do so and when I next fired I could not calculate my aim owing to the excitement. If I had been able to do so I should simply have disabled him and got away.

"After Dyson fell I rushed into the middle of the road and stood there for some moments. I hesitated as to what I should do. I felt disposed at first to go back and assist Dyson up, not thinking that he was wounded fatally, but I was labouring under great agitation, a number of people were gathering about. I heard them moving and rushing and, at last, I decided to fly."

Peace persisted for several hundred more words that he had never intended to kill Dyson and that there had been a struggle which Mrs. Dyson had witnessed. He continued:—

"During my life I have never once attempted to take life wilfully. I did not mean to take the life either of the Manchester policeman or of Mr. Dyson. Instead of taking life my object has been to save life.

"I have fired many hundreds of barrels at people to frighten them and I did succeed in frightening them and in getting away after I had done what I came to do. Where they have lost their lives has been when they have roused me, struggled with me and prevented my getting away and even then it has been in a scuffle and never intentionally. Of course I have used threats that I would shoot them, but that was only meant to frighten them also.

"My great mistake, sir, and I can see it as my end approaches has been this—in all my career I have used ball cartridges. I can now see that in using ball cartridges I did wrong. I ought to have used blank cartridge, then I would not have taken life".

Peace asked Mr. Littlewood to use his influence in Darnall to prevent people from persecuting members of his family. "They could not help anything I have done. They have no more to do with all my crimes than the greatest stranger in the land."

He added: "I hope God will give me strength to go like a hero to the scaffold. I do not say this, sir, in any sort of bravado. I do not mean a hero such as some persons will understand when they read this. I mean such a hero as my God might wish me to be. I feel penitent for all my crimes. I would atone for it to the utmost of my power, and I shall endeavour to die bravely."

Peace went on to suggest to Mr. Littlewood that he might preach a sermon in church at Darnall the Sunday after his execution, holding up his (Peace's) career as a beacon to others as to how not to live. He then asked the parson to hear him pray.

He was helped from his chair to his knees by his warders. Mr. Littlewood knelt and Peace asked the warders to kneel also. They agreed and Peace launched into a long prayer, asking help from God for himself, his family, Mr. Littlewood and his family, those he had wronged, the two men he had murdered, and for society generally. Altogether he prayed for something like twenty minutes.

He asked Mr. Littlewood if he should ask to see Mrs. Dyson so that he could ask her forgiveness, but Mr. Littlewood discouraged this idea. Finally Peace asked Mr. Littlewood to pray for him and sobbed incessantly, crying out repeatedly "God, have mercy upon me", throughout the Vicar's words.

When the parson was leaving Peace told him, "I pray we may meet again in Heaven". He then asked Mr. Littlewood to take the right hand of one of the warders, while he clasped the man's left hand. It was a way of shaking hands without violating the prison rule that he must not contact visitors.

It was perhaps as well that Peace did not ask to see Mrs. Dyson. That formidable woman was unrelenting in her hatred of him. She told reporters: "My opinion is that Peace is a perfect demon. I am told that since he has been sentenced to death he has become a changed character. That I don't believe. The place to which the wicked go is not bad enough for him. I think its occupants, bad as they might be, are too good to be where he is. No matter where he goes, I am satisfied there will be hell. Not even Shakespeare could adequately paint such a man as he has been. My life-long regret will be that I ever knew him."

She claimed that far from associating with Peace he had followed her about. She said that even the photograph showing them together at Sheffield Fair was not what it seemed. "I went to the Fair with a neighbour and her children, and when we got into the photographic studio my intention was to have the children photographed. I had no intention whatever of having myself taken with Peace, but he stood behind my chair at the time my likeness was taken. That was quite unknown to me though at the time."

She continued to reiterate that she had never written to Peace in her life, that the letters found dropped by Peace in the field after her husband was shot were forgeries, concocted by Peace to discredit her, and that she had certainly not been with him the night before her husband was killed. She said that she had received threats from Sheffield to dissuade her from returning from America to give evidence against Peace, but that she would have done so, "If I had to walk on my head all the way."

Whatever the situation in those early days at Darnall; whether or not a tempted Mrs. Dyson did sneak into the garret of the empty house between their two homes to meet Peace; did rollick "slightly inebriated" through the night streets of Sheffield with him; did answer to recognised signals from the white-whiskered little man who was so obsessed with her, one thing in the end was certain. Catherine Dyson came to hate Peace with a deep and bitter hatred so great that she risked reputation, even perhaps safety itself at the hands of his criminal friends, submitted to public odium—she was hooted in the streets of Sheffield—to see that he went to the gallows. We can know that absolutely. What other emotions he stirred in her at other times can only be surmised.

Peace's confession raised one important point. It does suggest that at the end, when he knew only death lay ahead, he abandoned the story that he had met Mrs. Dyson the day before he shot her husband. Indeed another version of his confession states that he returned to Sheffield the morning after the Habron trial, which would have made the alleged meeting in the Stag Hotel impossible. Without the original taken down by the Rev. Littlewood the exact phrasing is lost. Neither version, in any case, mentions such a meeting. Peace would have enjoyed fooling Mr. Dyson by meeting his wife secretly behind his back. He would surely not have become as insanely jealous of the railway engineer as he obviously did become. In any case if he was still so friendly with Mrs. Dyson why did he not persuade her to withdraw the summons *which was in her name* without telling her husband. No, Peace's rage was that of the man of his calibre spurned by a woman. To a man like Peace nothing would be more dreadful than to be told by a woman she had tired of him—before he had tired of her.

Finally, there is the significant clue that Peace had cut off Mrs. Dyson's credit with the Halfway House hotel. He would hardly have done that to a mistress from whom he was still expecting favours.

Of Peace's confession one final thing must be said. The newspapers of his time, and even police experts, have claimed that Peace committed several murders in the course of his career, but these could not be proved.

It is a difficult point. The police records on Peace are not now available. On the other hand Peace, at the end, had no reason to hold anything back. He even admitted he had fired "many hundreds of barrels" at people during his career. There was no reason why he should not have made a clean breast of all his crimes.

His courage did not fail him. He drew from somewhere a strength of mind that was to enable him—as William Marwood the official executioner was later to agree—to face death with the greatest calm. He prepared his Will. He told his brother,

Dan, during a visit that his property was mostly furniture and some shares in the London Tramway Corporation. "I am worth about £550", he observed. On the 24th, the day before his death, he signed the Will, leaving everything he had equally to Willie and his daughter, Jane Ann, "free from the control and debts of her present or any future husband."

The day was spent in seeing visitors. Mrs. Peace, Willie and Jane and her husband, William Bolsover, with their baby, were allowed in at midday. Peace was writing at his table. He said he was feeling weak, but otherwise in good spirits. The two warders assisted him to move to a chair near the bars separating him from the little party. For a while there was a silence as the visitors strove to control their emotions. Peace spoke first and told them he did not wish them to be distressed.

The little party talked for some time. While they were doing so there was the sound of hammering from the courtyard. Peace listened for a moment and then said: "I hear they are working on my scaffold. I have heard them before this morning."

The Chief Warder cut in: "You are mistaken, Peace."

Peace gave a smile. "I am not. I have worked so long with wood I know the sound of deal, and they don't have deal in prisons for anything else than for scaffolds. I have heard them knocking in the nails and I am sure that I am right." He was.

He added: "It makes no difference to me. I should like to see my own coffin and my own grave. I am prepared. I only look upon the scaffold as a short cut to Heaven. I shall be thrown into my grave like a dog, but it won't matter. It will only be my poor body that will be there. My soul, I believe, will be in Heaven."

Peace told his family that he intended to write them last letters. His hands, he said, would be tied behind him on his way to the scaffold. He would hold the letters in his hands and ask the Chaplain to take them at the last minute and see to it that they were received by the people for whom they were intended.

After three hours the time came for the family to leave. He asked each member of the family if they wished individually to say anything to him. The answers were sobs. Peace begged them not to break down and asked if they would all pray with him. Peace asked his warders to help him to kneel.

While the party kneeled Peace prayed for half-an-hour, praying for each member of his family in turn. He prayed for young Habron and for others he had wronged. It was only when his relatives rose to leave that for the first time Peace's iron will cracked. He was allowed as a final concession to touch hands with each member of the party, and embrace his wife and daughter. He broke down for a few moments, but was able to control himself again in time to bid the final farewells.

The rest of the day he spent writing the letters he had promised. He had quite recovered his composure and there was a flash of the old Peace, when, after a bout of coughing, he turned to his warders and asked: "Do you think Marwood can cure this cough of mine?"

Included in his letter to his wife was a funeral memorial card he had prepared himself. It read:—

In Memory of Charles Peace
who was executed in Armley Prison
Tuesday, February 25th, 1879
Aged 47.
For that I don but never intended.

He wrote to William Bolsover: "This is my last letter here on earth. Let me beg of you to take my dreadful end as a warning . . ." and concluded, "I am gone to Heaven. Goodbye, Charles Peace."

Little is known of the fate of the family after Peace's death. Mrs. Peace continued to live with her daughter and son-in-law at Darnall until she died in 1891. Willie appeared for "one-night only" at the Gaiety Theatre, Barnsley, as a performer, playing the concertina and answering questions put to him about Peace. The career of Willie Ward as a music hall artist does not seem to have prospered. The novelty was not repeated.

After Peace had written his letters he slept for a while until about 11 p.m. The Governor of the prison came to see him and to him Peace made a request that he might speak to Marwood before the execution. He appeared agitated on this point and finally the Governor agreed that it would be arranged. The Governor left and Peace prayed and talked with the Prison

Chaplain until two o'clock. He then became drowsy and fell asleep.

Peace slept soundly until quarter to six. He breakfasted and made a hearty meal of toast and tea and bacon and eggs. He seemed stronger than he had for some days and munched away composedly. Though he did remark to his warders, "bloody poor bacon, this". After breakfast he retired to the lavatory recess. He was a longish while inside and one of the warders, becoming nervous, knocked on the door and asked him how long he was going to be.

"You're in a hell of a hurry. Who's going to be hanged this morning, you or me," Peace growled.

The night had been clear though bitterly cold. A crowd had begun to gather outside the walls of the prison from midnight onwards and by seven had grown to a thousand people.

At quarter-to-eight Marwood, in response to a request by the Governor, went to Peace's cell. He said later: "He had got hold of the idea that I should terribly punish him at the scaffold. As I entered the condemned cell—which was about 100 yards from the scaffold—Peace was seated. He was in convict dress. The bandage had been removed from his head. He was neither weak nor prostrate, but sat upright in his chair as though he had never known a moment's illness. When I appeared at the door he appeared pleased and holding out his hand, said 'I am glad to see you, Mr. Marwood. I wish to have a word with you. I do hope you will not punish me. I hope you will do your work quickly.' 'You shall not suffer pain from my hand,' I replied, and then Peace, grasping my arm, said, 'God Bless you. I hope to meet you all in Heaven. I am thankful all my sins are forgiven.'

"It was now time to pinion him. He stood at my request, but did not really need the support of two warders by his side. He was not at all nervous and quietly submitted to my operations. Pinioning is a very ingenious process. I run a main strap round the body, and connected with it are two other straps, which take the small of the arm, so that the elbows are fastened close to the body and the hands are free. Peace complained 'the straps fit very tight'. I replied 'it is better so. It will prevent you from suffering!'

"Taking hold of the main strap, so as to keep my hand on him, we started for the scaffold . . ."

The dreadful procession to the scaffold, which had been erected in the courtyard of the prison near the high wall, wound out of the cell, the Governor and the Under-Sheriff of the County leading, followed by the Chaplain, Peace behind him with two warders on either side, Marwood just behind Peace and two ranks of warders bringing up the rear.

The prison bell began to toll and the Chaplain to read the Burial Service. As they emerged into the courtyard snow was falling. Peace's face was pinched from the cold, but he did not seem afraid. He looked round him keenly.

The scaffold was painted black and the lower-part draped in black cloth, and Peace had to walk some distance in full sight of this dreadful apparatus. He stepped out resolutely. Twice he nearly missed his footing on the icy pathway, but the warders were there to see he did not fall. They helped him up the steps and stood him beneath the noose dangling from the crossbar overhead. Marwood took the rope down and prepared to put the white cap over Peace's head. "Stop a minute," Peace said, "let me hear this." He stood listening to the Chaplain conclude the prayers and then spoke, "Oh God, have mercy upon me. Oh Christ, have mercy upon me."

Again Marwood tried to adjust the white cap and rope, but Peace turned his head and said: "I want to speak." He proceeded to address the little company of newspapermen in a clear, firm voice, which carried to the crowd over the prison wall.

"You gentlemen reporters, I wish you to notice the few words I am going to say. You know what my life has been. It has been base; and had I wished to ask the world, after you have seen my death, what man could die as I die if he did not die in the fear of the Lord. Tell all my friends that I feel sure that they sincerely forgive me and that I am going into the Kingdom of Heaven, or else to that place prepared for us to rest until the day of judgement. I have no enemies that I feel anything against on earth. I wish that all my enemies would do so to me. I wish them well. I wish them to come to the Kingdom of Heaven at last. Amen. Say that my last respects is to my dear children and to their dear mother. I hope that no paper will disgrace itself by taunting them and jeering at them on my account, but will have mercy upon them. God Bless You, my dear children. To each of my children goodbye and Heaven bless you. Goodbye and Amen."

Marwood drew the white cap over Peace's head and began to adjust the rope to his neck. Peace turned his head slightly and demanded, "I should like to have a drink." His request was ignored. Marwood was working as fast as he could. Peace spoke again: "The rope fits very tight." Marwood told him: "Never mind. It is all for the best. Hold up your chin. I won't hurt you." Peace did as he was told. "Goodbye and God Bless you All," he said. He started again: "Goodbye and God Bless . . ." Marwood slammed the lever forward. The platform swung open and Peace plummeted down. Nine feet four inches down he came to the end of the rope. A small man gets a long drop.

After it had hung for an hour, as the Law demands, Peace's body was cut down and interred unceremoniously in the prison yard. Back in the Condemned Cell the gas was still burning. On the bed was the Bible and a Prayer Book. Peace's slippers were by the bed. On the table were several sheets of paper, one an unfinished letter. . . .

* * *

The times that made Charles Peace have gone. The Sheffield of Charlie Peace has almost passed away. There, as in every other great town, the huge cliffs of the new concrete buildings are beginning to sprout upwards from the black huddled dwellings of the earlier, and grimmer, industrial past. There are still, however, in the Northern towns streets where Charlie Peace would feel at home. On a dark winter night, in these places, it is possible to imagine a small agile figure slipping furtively along, and to see in the light of the street lamps that white-whiskered face and the dark eyes gleaming with something that might be diabolic humour, or plain ferocious murder.